Flying With My Higher Self

Flying With My Higher Self

Awakening to Self-Mastery

Robert R. Maldonado, PhD

Also by Robert Maldonado

Children of Atlantis—Keepers of the Crystal Skull

The Calling of the Heart—A Journey in Self-Healing

available from Amazon.com
and at
www.authorrobertmaldonado.com

FLYING WITH MY HIGHER SELF
Awakening to Self-Mastery
By Robert R. Maldonado, PhD

All rights reserved. This book, or parts thereof, may not be reproduced in any form without written permission from the publisher.

ISBN: 0997208317
ISBN-13: 9780997208313

Copyright
February 28, 2018
Cover Artist:
Designcrowd.com

Publishing, and Page Layout by
Visions of Reality
PO Box 277
Chalfont, PA 18914
WEBSITE: www.new-visions.com
215-996-0646

Printed in the United States of America

Dedication

*This book is dedicated to Archangel Gabriel
for her guidance and inspiration.*

*To my Blessed Higher Self.
Without his presence in my life as a guide and helper,
I could not have written this book.*

*To all of those beautiful souls who are "flying" with their higher self,
keep soaring and trust that your path is unfolding as it is meant to be.*

Here is the test to find whether your mission on earth is finished: If you're alive, it isn't.

—Jonathan Bach

We have all a better guide in ourselves, if we would attend to it, wiser than any other person can be.

—Jane Austen

"Helicopters are different from planes. An airplane by its nature wants to fly and if not interfered to strongly by unusual events or by a deliberately incompetent pilot, it will fly. A helicopter does not want to fly. It is maintained in the air by a variety of forces and controls working in opposition to each other; and, if there is any disturbance in the delicate balance, the helicopter stops flying immediately and disastrously. There is no such thing as a gliding helicopter. This is why being a helicopter pilot is so different from being an airplane pilot; and why, in generality, airplane pilots are open, clear-eyed, buoyant extroverts and helicopter pilots are brooders, introspective anticipators of trouble. They know that if something bad has not happened, it is about to."

—Harry Reasoner, ABC Evening News

Walk the middle road because,
If you choose to center,
And do not participate in
The extreme, disruptive energies,
You will come to know God.

—E. Joyce – 6/19/2014

Do not be conformed to this world, but be transformed by the renewing of your minds, so that you may discern what is the will of God.

—Romans 12:2

Table of Contents

Dedication ·vii
Photographs · xiii
Acknowledgements ·xv
Foreword ·xvii
Introduction · xix

I · 1
II · 9
III ·21
IV ·25
V ·29
VI ·35
VII ·47
VIII · 55
IX ·61
X ·71
XI · 77
XII · 83
XIII ·89
XIV · 97
XV · 101
XVI ·107

XVII	111
XVIII	115
XIX	119
XX	125
XXI	135
XXII	139
XXIII	145
Epilogue	149
Resources	151
Glossary	153
Website References	157
Archangel Gabriel	161
Your Higher Self	163
About The Author Robert R. Maldonado, PhD	165

Photographs

Pastel Picture of Helicopter
Flight Manual Cover
Manual Table of Contents
Whirlybird Poster
Operating Procedures
Principal Dimensions & Instruments
Instruments
Feather
Constant Heading Square
PAVELOW Doing Hoist Recovery
Straight-in Autorotation to Hover
Running Landing
Vertical Landing
Quick Stop Procedure
Traffic Pattern
Rescue Operations
Engine Failure At Altitude
Operating Limitations
Bob & Helicopter

Acknowledgements

In truth, my Higher Self is really the author of this book. He is the one who suggested that the book be written, proposing the right concepts and understanding for the reader at this time in the evolution of humanity.

I owe a huge debt of gratitude to my wife Ellen for her loving support, encouragement and wonderful insights. You are the love of my life.

To Judy Bishop Woods for her fantastic editing and detailed suggestions after many iterations.

To Elizabeth Joyce for her friendship, guidance, and inspiration in the creation of this book, and for reminding me of my own mastery.

To Teresa Brown for her wonderful encouragement and who predicted that this book would one day be written.

To all the members of my meditation group for your unfailing support and showing me the way.

To my family of *Star Seeds* of the group of forty who have inspired me to a path in planetary healing and higher consciousness.

To thank the reader for your interest and taking the time to read this book. May you be blessed by the words and appreciate the amazing and loving support of your higher self.

Foreword

I was delighted to hear that Robert Maldonado had completed this special book.

I know he understands, from experience, the difficulties for all of us as we "follow the Path" from one level of awareness into the next. The new generations of children are born with the innate knowledge that we cannot survive without a direct connection to the Divine and All-that-IS. They are immersed in this energy as a natural part of life here on Earth.

Which of us, upon taking up the study of yoga or meditation, have not felt the reproach from old friends and family members? Have we not felt guilt, or even worse, felt that we were some kind of deserters for not staying "true" to organized religion or the rules of society?

These are common feelings, but they are not written about much except by great teachers and gurus. There are gems in this book, and I love Robert's analogy of people on Earth being like a helicopter. None of us know who we will be sitting next to in an airplane, or the extent a helicopter pilot goes to when saving others.

Whoever these people are, for the moment, they have been brought together for a purpose; whether it's to fly to a location, or to save a life. Yet, for these moments, they are overlapping auras, extending an arm of safety, and in those moments may realize that we all have to get along. Now we are reading this book, filled with living examples of loving and honoring others, and we are feeling and absorbing the wisdom brought to us by the author.

Robert R. Maldonado, PhD

This is timely work and much appreciated: As we quickly approach the difficult 2020's, it is not just us as individuals who are seeking a greater understanding, but the Earth herself seems to be "kicking up a storm," or two. Robert shows us that it is not enough to know about the benefits of merging with our *Blessed Higher Self*, but we must grow, align, and readjust our own faults, judgments, and criticisms, while continuing this merging.

As we progress further and further into the higher realms of the Universe, we have less and less of the old world to hang on to — the world as we know it is disappearing, and in its place we are finally beginning to experience balance, kindness, love, peace, and harmony. Only those who open their eyes, auras, and hearts and *see* will move along with the tides of change and survive.

If you are open to learning, understanding, and accessing the inner dimensions of your SELF, then this book — *Flying With My Higher Self* — is for you. Besides being an excellent teacher and healer, Robert walks the path he so beautifully writes about.

—Elizabeth Joyce
Spiritual Teacher
www.new-visions.com
October 7, 2017

Introduction

After writing my first novel, *Children of Atlantis: Keepers of the Crystal Skull*, I knew that I'd write again, but unsure of what about. The book's premise was to bring a new awareness around the energies at work in the final hours of ancient Atlantis as it relates to the inner and outer struggles we face on the spiritual path, and how to transform ourselves with love, honesty and acceptance. Like that effort, I was looking for something as inspirational and transformative, yet that fit what was needed in these challenging and changing times.

One morning, as I sat comfortably in the quiet space of my office overlooking the bay, I closed my eyes and asked with a sincere heart, "What am I being asked to share now?" The answer came in a soft, calm voice that I recognized, *"Why don't you tell them about US?"* It was as if my pen was coming alive in my hand and writing by itself as I scribbled on the yellow pad the words *"Why don't you tell them about US?"*

The *US* was me and my blessed Higher Self; a personal friend and confidant who loves me unconditionally and knows me better than I do. He's always encouraging and positive and has the answers, when I care to listen. In his own gentle way, and with a playful sense of humor, he reminds me that he IS the very essence of who I am and that WE are connected for eternity. He holds all the accumulated knowledge from all my lifetimes, communicates by sending odd coincidences and synchronicities, new insights, suggestions and expanded awareness, and above all, understanding. Most importantly, he leads me to all the things I need to do to grow spiritually.

I call him "he" because in this life that's how I see him. But, I know "he" transcends gender. I have come to understand that all of us are having a conversation with our Higher Self at some time, asking for guidance, help, insight and assistance. That's in fact the purpose of this book, to invite the reader to experience a new and more personal relationship with their Higher Self and to keep the dialogue going during these dramatic and exciting times. Spiritual growth as described here means growing through connecting with your Higher Self and becoming our Higher Self, a being of light, so that we can fulfill our life purpose.

As I glanced at what I had written, I wondered how to convey this to my reading audience. After all, I considered the "US" a work in progress with not much to say, yet.

It's not for you to wonder, 'Why.' You teach best what you need most to learn!

Okay. I get it. I am still learning how this works, right. So, what do you want me to say about US? I asked. Then, unexpectedly, later that night in a dream, I got a hint of what was to come.

> Once upon a time, a helicopter pilot heard a voice tell him of an ancient and beautiful city of light in another dimension. It was reachable the voice assured him. Curiously, the pilot would fly, most days, to where he thought the city might be only to have to turn back.
>
> Many times, he saw what appeared to be lights in the distance but couldn't get there. Bad weather or lack of fuel forced him to return home. Soon he began to doubt the voice, yet, he trusted enough to keep trying.
>
> One day after flying over a huge, mountainous wilderness surrounded by miles of sheer cliffs, unstable glaciers, and turbulent canyon rivers, he saw it: an ancient city hidden among the trees glowing in a shimmering white light. It was magnificent.
>
> Thrilled, he landed and was joyously met by its inhabitants. As he explored, he saw evidence of fabulous wealth—gold and gems, fields

of grain and fruit, works of art, libraries, hospitals, intricate machines and other wonders. Everyone appeared to be living in harmony.

The pilot felt as if he had arrived home after a very long absence. The people taught him about higher states of consciousness, his fifth dimensional body and how to use concepts/technologies such as bi-location, thought projection, telepathy, and astral travel.

He could not wait to share this discovery with his family and friends. Once home, he told his girlfriend about it, but she demurred, saying she was afraid of flying.

Another friend, also skeptical, said "Well, OKAY, I am not sure if this is real or imagined, but that city sounds kind of interesting." But he never found the time to go.

The pilot approached many people, telling them of the fabulous city, but could not find anyone to fly with him no matter how hard he tried.

Then, one day he heard a call in the wilderness of space-time from someone who was trying hard to listen and trust the wisdom of his higher self-guidance. Excited, the helicopter pilot thought that maybe, just maybe, this time, he had found someone to fly with him after all.

The pilot took his new friend to the city of light and taught him everything he knew including how to fly, and they became the best of friends. And in time, the pilot's friend became like the pilot, a master teacher sharing with others the lessons on the spiritual path.

The dream made me wonder what it would be like to meet an ascended master, or highly evolved being like Jesus or a Buddha, who could *take ME to the City of Light*. What would he or she say and be like? What if we could have a personal conversation and I could ask *anything,* and get answers to all my questions. This being could guide me on my spiritual path and explain things like how the world of duality works, and about the higher dimensions; how to manifest, and how to realize my higher self and be in my own light. Wow, I could ask how to realize my full potential and, maybe, even get a glimpse of the future.

Robert R. Maldonado, PhD

Perhaps it's no coincidence that you are holding this book in your hands; perhaps there is something in these pages for you to acknowledge and remember.

Then, one day, my wish was granted, and this book was born.

Robert R. Maldonado
November, 2017

Pastel Painting of Bell Helicopter

I

I am a perfect expression of God's love, here and now.

I met Sam Watson on a hot summer morning and it changed my life. The local airport was hosting an air show that included the Confederate Air Force and its collection of World War II era warbirds along with the Coast Guard, Civil Air Patrol and other flying organizations from around the state. I love airplanes, grew up with them and flew them in my military career. Thinking back, Sam was much the same.

It was a beautiful day with a slight breeze out of the south in a cloudless blue sky in small town Alabama-- great flying weather I thought. I slowly walked around the tarmac admiring the different aircraft— a Boeing B-17 Flying Fortress *Good Conduct*, B-24 Liberator *Sally B,* with over 50 combat missions stenciled below the cockpit, and a rare North American P-51 Mustang fighter, its refurbished silver fuselage gleaming in the sunlight. It was impressive. There was even a Civil Air Patrol Cessna 180, Coast Guard HH-65A Dauphin rescue chopper and an enormous U.S. Navy MH-53E minesweeper helicopter.

There were a lot of people milling around admiring the displays. Overhead a bright red biplane recalling the Red Baron of World War I fame was performing loops and rolls with a man perched atop of the wing. I thought to myself—now that takes some guts.

Then I noticed him. An elderly man about my height and size with wispy white hair, deep tan, and lively brown eyes shaded by a worn baseball cap. From a distance, he appeared to glow. I always thought that white hair suggested understanding and wisdom—seasoning. Well, this guy had it.

As I wandered over his way, I felt a sense of contagious calm. This guy exuded a quiet confidence about him. I liked that.

He was leaning against the side of a Bell 47 helicopter that looked like something I had seen in a 50's TV series, "The Whirlybirds," which was about the adventures of duo "PT" and Chuck, the pilots. In case you were wondering, growing up, PT and Chuck were my heroes. I wanted to be just like them flying their helicopter and helping people. Who would have guessed I would also become a "whirlybird" pilot later in life, but that's another story.

He had just finished talking with a young woman and then turned to face me. He gave me a quick glance as if he was expecting me.

"Hey" I said extending my hand. "I used to love these things," nodding toward the aircraft.

He returned my smile with a firm but warm handshake and said, "Sam Watson, I still do love it."

"Hi Sam, I'm Robert."

"Well, nice to meet you, Robert."

"You too. Where you from?"

"Oh…everywhere…do lots of traveling, no place to call home."

"First time here?"

"No. Been here a few times, always liked it." I nodded, looking at the helicopter. "Look, Sam, somehow I felt I needed to come by…" *Shoot, where did that come from?*

"I know." He paused after seeing the look on my face. *What did he mean by that, I wondered.*

"Care to have a look?" He nodded his head in the direction of the helicopter.

Noticing other people peering inside the cockpit, "Yes, I'd love that, but I don't want to interrupt you."

Flying With My Higher Self

He just smiled. "Come on!"

We turned to the helicopter. It was a white 1954 Bell Model 47G-2 so clean looking it was as if it had just left the factory. Even smelled new. In the cockpit, the instrument panel looked factory original and I noticed a mint condition leather seat, and the dual set of controls with right hand cyclic control stick, and collective pitch lever-throttle control. The cockpit window sparkled which was strange with all the bugs we have around here, but this one didn't even have a scratch on it. The metal blades looked new with factory abrasion strips still installed. Even the tie-down ropes looked new. I was wondering if this guy had recently built it from a kit. Then it hit me: there were no leaks. That's odd. Every flying helicopter has at some time leaked. We used to have a saying that if it did not "bleed" it was not worthy to be flown.

As I patted the fuselage I asked nonchalantly, "What kind of flying you do Sam?"

He grinned, "I offer rides."

I nodded, running my hand over the aircraft's metal. "With the dual control package, you must offer lessons." I felt a twinge of eagerness at the idea.

"Yes, I do. I'm taking applications Robert. The first one is free. After that if you are still interested, its $200 for five rides. A bargain, if I may say so." He smiled an easy smile.

On the white fuel tank behind the cockpit, I read the name *Gabriel* painted in gold in a distinctive script. All that was missing was a picture above the name like the nose art of old World War II war birds.

"Sam...who's Gabriel?" I asked.

"A dear friend, Robert."

I smiled. "I would like to get a ride on Gabriel, sometime. How's your schedule look?"

"Open. How about tomorrow morning, say 9 a.m.? I am hanging around awhile after the air show to give some local flights."

"Sounds good." I said, nodding in agreement. I felt the happy inner child in me coming to life, again.

I continued walking around Gabriel and Sam followed, watching me closely. It was those eyes again, deep and penetrating and yet welcoming. I felt as if I knew him from somewhere. Where? So familiar and I couldn't place it. He walked in easy graceful strides; and almost had an iridescent glow as he faded in and out of the sun.

"How long have you had Gabriel, Sam? She's spotless."

"A long time…let's see. First got her from the factory in 1954. She was beautiful… love at first sight."

That's as old as I am, I thought. I should look so good.

"Any problems?"

"Just the usual, you know, otherwise she's been running great."

I did some rough calculating in my head. That's over 60 years. Like the human body, all aircraft have a useful life span set by the manufacturer typically in cycles or flight hours. It's rare to find any aircraft let alone a helicopter that has flown more than 50 years—the Boeing B-52 Bomber still flying missions in Afghanistan came to mind as the exception. Of course, it gets overhauled routinely. There were exceptions. The Sikorsky CH-53 that I flew first came off the line in 1966 and versions of it are still flying. So, it was possible.

I noticed a young father with his son waiting for a look and moved to make room for them. "Thanks Sam. See you tomorrow…9 a.m., right?"

He smiled. "Great. Hold on a moment, Robert."

He turned and walked to the cockpit and reaching in the baggage space behind the seat pulled out a big black book.

"Here…a little light reading to acquaint you with the 47." He chuckled.

I laughed as he hefted it over to me. "Thanks." I glanced at the title, *Flight Manual Bell Helicopter Model 47G-2, December 31, 1954.*

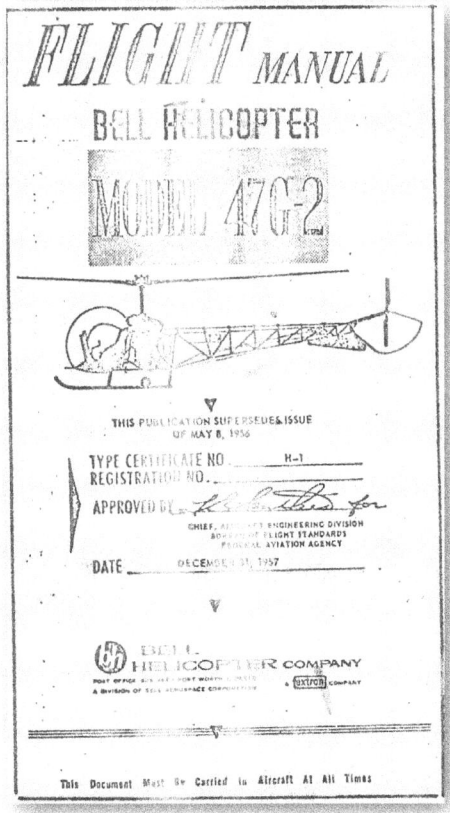

Cover of Flight Manual

On my way home, I felt as if something within me had shifted, opened up after meeting Sam. I couldn't explain it. It was a subtle feeling that my rational mind couldn't find words to describe. That always happens, because the mind cannot always comprehend what the heart *feels*. I chalked it up to my excitement at the prospect of flying in the morning. New challenges always lifted me.

That evening, comfortably settled on my sofa, I took out the manual. The pages were stained and yellowed and visibly worn from usage and time. The table of contents looked pretty standard with operating limitations, procedures, performance data, and charts and tables. The newer manuals that I was familiar with had hundreds of pages of cautions, warnings, complex procedures, and start-up sequences – chock full of charts and change orders. Not this one. Simple, yet thorough. As I thumbed through it I felt as if I was going back in time, flying an antique compared to the turbine-powered models I was familiar with. The child in me was jumping for joy and screaming, *we're going to fly in a real whirlybird!* Yes, a real whirlybird! Never done that before. P.T. and Chuck would be proud! I was smiling to myself.

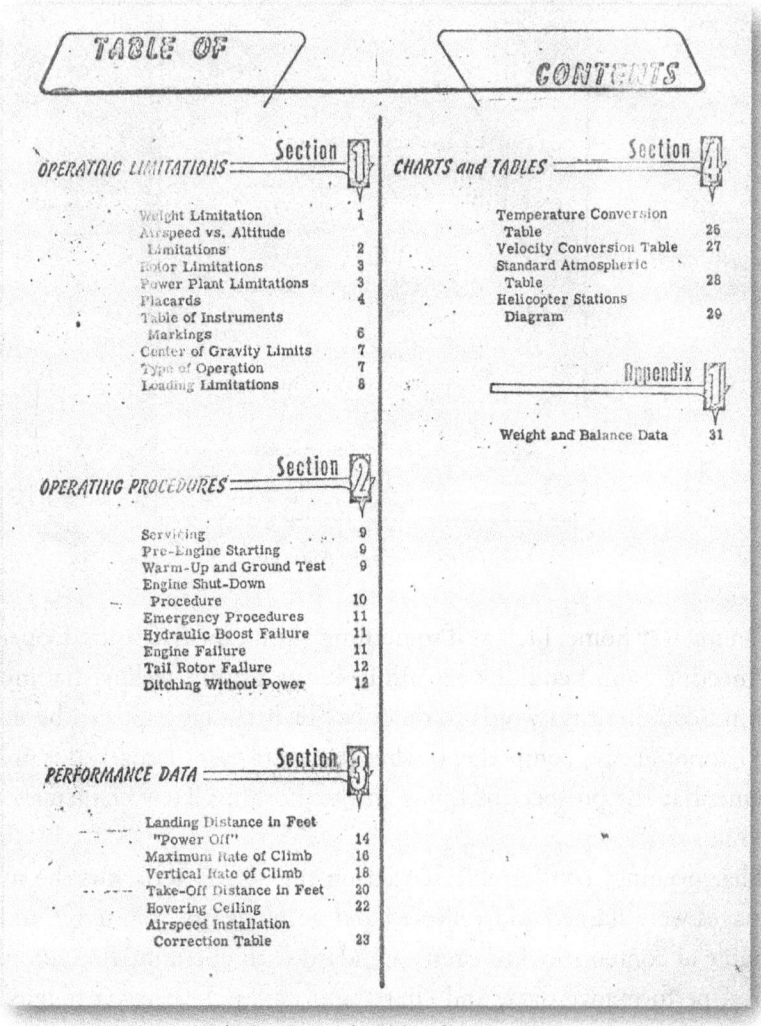

Flight Manual Table of Contents

Flying With My Higher Self

"Whirlybirds" movie photo

As I flipped through the manual, and yes, I wanted to be prepared for Sam, a section in the back caught my attention. The hand-written tab read *"Reminders for the God-Fearing Helicopter Pilot on the Spiritual Path."* Behind it was a small handbook tucked away in the back pocket labeled *"Ascension Handbook."* It was scribbled with lines crossed out and had what appeared to be sayings or maxims throughout the margin. Different, I thought. A few phrases jumped out at me, but the biggest surprise was seeing my name "Robert" at the top, followed by random quotes:

> *Robert,*
> *You are a master. Act like one...*
> *Flying is an extension of your mastery of self...*
> *Be proud of your achievements for they are precious fortunes in the changing chapters of your life...*
> *No matter what happens, no matter how difficult the circumstances, I will give you the peace that passes all understanding. It is only for you to trust me...*
> *Be grateful for the gift that you are to the world...*

Whoa. My breath caught. This was some weird synchronicity going on. Over the past few years, well, since leaving the military, I'd taken different paths sort of exploring my spirituality, healing, and various metaphysical practices. It was a personal quest to grow on the spiritual path.

I looked at the page again. The words echoed in my head. I closed the manual, wondering who this Robert was.

II

*Someday I'm going to meet a person who never faced a test.
I'll ask, "What are you doing here?"*

—Richard Bach

I showed up at the airport at 8:50 am, ready to go. Sam was already doing the preflight inspection. The flying dream I had the night before was still in my mind.

"Good morning, Sam. How're you doing?"

Looking over his shoulder as he stooped to untie the helicopter, "Good morning to you, sir. A beautiful day."

"That it is."

"Got more folks to sign up for rides?" as I noticed a few people milling around the nearby hangar door.

"A few yesterday. None today. Just us, Robert. Hope that's okay. Grab this, will you?" As he handed me the tie down rope and climbed onto the skid, checking the swash-plate and controls.

"Sam, I was thinking. I know nothing about you… your flying background, anything."

He smiled, "Are you worried?"

"No, just interested. How'd you get into this?"

He glanced down at me and smiling said, "You mean flying?"

"Right."

He climbed down and walked to the rear while shaking the elevator, as if examining my question. "Hmmm…I see. Trust is important."

"Yes, you could say that. Is there a mystery here?" I blurted out.

"Let's just say that I was well trained."

The conversation had taken an unexpected turn. You know, I looked you up on the internet, LinkedIn and Facebook and couldn't find you anywhere. There's nothing on a Sam Watson, pilot, anywhere."

"Oh, you won't find me there," he said casually.

"I see. You do have a license… right?"

He rounded to the cockpit and, reaching behind the seat, pulled out a certificate that looked just as worn as the flight manual.

UNITED STATES OF AMERICA
DEPARTMENT OF TRANSPORTATION
FEDERAL AVIATION ADMINSTRATION

IV. NAME: Sam Watson
V. ADDRESS: Anywhere
VI. NATIONALITY: USA
VI a. DOB: 10/03/1934 SEX: M HEIGHT: 5 ft. 10 in, WEIGHT: 177 lbs., HAIR: BRWN, EYES: BRWN

HAS BEEN QUALIFIED TO EXERCISE THE PRIVILEGES OF

I. COMMERCIAL PILOT BELL 47G-2, INSTRUCTOR/EVALUATOR
II. CERTIFICATE NUMBER: H-1
III. DATE OF ISSUE: 09/06/1957

It looked legitimate. I handed it back to him with a sheepish smile. "Thanks. I just …, You must have been precocious to buy an aircraft right off the line like that." I left just a slight question in my voice.

Laughing, "Precocious alright. Ready to fly, Robert? Preflight's done—a few things to point out, besides you already know about how to do a preflight, am I right?"

"Well… yeah… hmmm."

He smiled as we walked around, and pointed as he started talking.

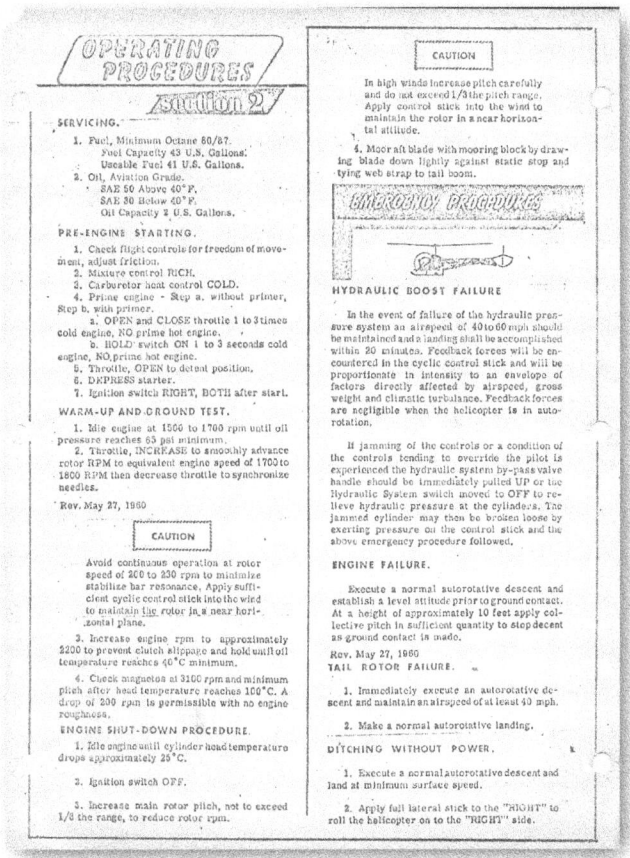

Operating Procedures

"There are a few items unique to the Bell 47-G-that I look for. I usually do a quick look-over making sure nothing is out of the ordinary. Found a bird nest nestled between my tanks once. Mama bird was not happy when I moved her. I make sure that the pitot tube cover is removed and blade tie downs removed and stowed."

Sam pulled the tie down rope from my hand.

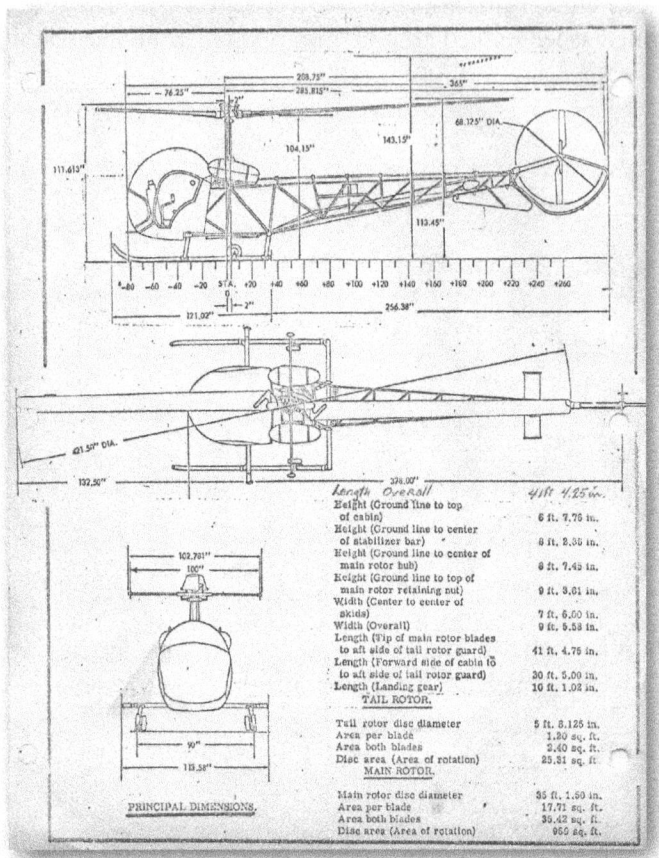

Principal Dimensions

"I like to move the blade to the front—gives me an idea where it is during start and for clearance. I have a measuring stick to check fuel level—pretty rudimentary, but lots of times the fuel gauge may "stick." I always go with what's in the tanks."

He climbed on the side to the tank, removed the caps and pulled the stick out. He checked it, held it up so I could see it, and nodded.

He peeked into the cockpit.

"I also look in the cockpit and make sure the avionics on top of the instrument panel are switched off. Hydraulic switch–off, carb switch-off and mag switches-off. We don't want these to drain the battery…," he paused. "Questions?"

"I noticed there was no preflight checklist in the manual."

"Good catch. The checklist was eventually included in subsequent models."

"Right… subsequent models?"

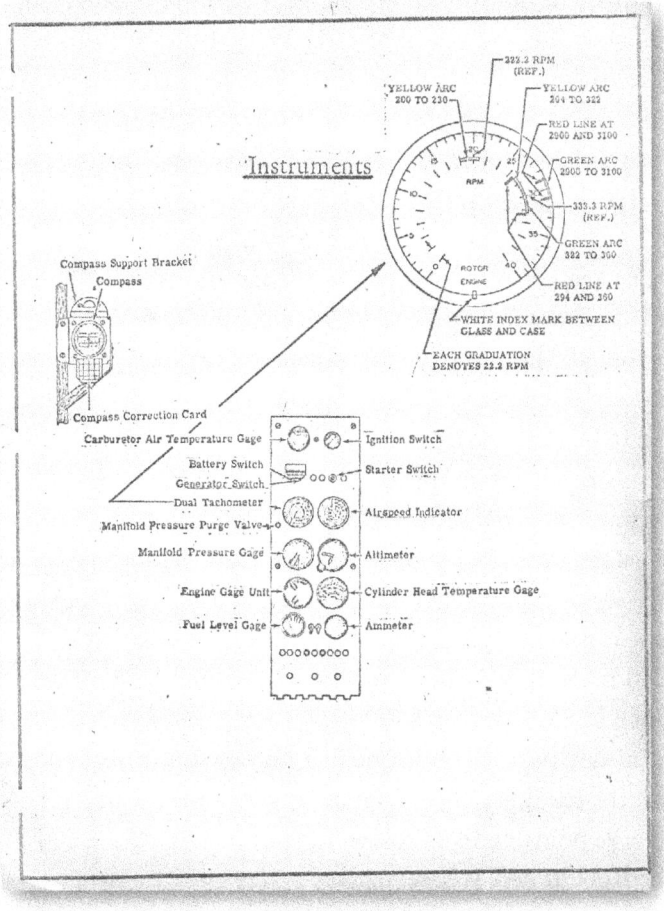

Instruments

Sam nodded and proceeded to tell me about the Bell 47 helicopter, design and development, operational history, civilian and military variants, and conversions as if he was a Bell factory representative. He said he had been a technical consultant on the TV M.A.S.H. series. Afterwards, I thought to myself there is no one on this planet that knows more about the Bell 47 than this guy. I was amazed at the depth of Sam's knowledge.

"Hey Sam, as I was leafing through the flight manual last night, I found this." I pulled out the scribbled paper from the back of the manual. I felt a little strange bringing it up.

"I couldn't help but notice my name at the top. Coincidence? Some of them resonated with my life right now. What I mean is, well, I don't know but I'd like to know more about this. Was he a student of yours?" I was floundering.

Sam just picked it up like it was normal exchange. "Yes, as a matter of fact. We stay in touch occasionally."

"I see. Well, let me give this back to you."

"No, just keep it." He removed his ball cap and ran his fingers through his white hair. "I expect that you and he are alike in many ways."

Sam grinned. "Let's go. We can talk about it some more later. Hop in."

We moved back toward the helicopter and I got in on right passenger side. It felt good to be back in the cockpit.

"Make sure you are strapped in," pointing to the seat belts. I'd already pulled the straps over my shoulders.

"The helmet is behind you, a little different than what you are probably used to, has a voice activated mike feature, reading light, form fit with latest technology. Has a nice visor, too."

I pulled it on; it was white and fit beautifully, a vast improvement over older models.

Sam finished putting on his helmet and strapped his kneeboard around his leg with the checklist, field diagram and frequency card and began to read off items while pointing them to me.

"Okay, Robert, here we are. Can you hear me?"

"Loud and clear.

Flying With My Higher Self

"Great, now we're ready for the pre-start and engine start checklist. Just follow me; you know the drill."

"Okay."

"Engine Start Checklist. I'll read the checklist item, carry out the function and say the response, as required. Just follow me and check it also. Got it?"

"No problem."

We fell into an easy rhythm, statement and check. Felt like being back home again.

Blade tie down—"REMOVED."

Fuel caps secure—"CHECKED," (checked on preflight).

Seat belt---"FASTENED," (pilot and passenger), as he leaned over and yanked on mine to check it.

Passenger brief- "Okay, in case of emergency.... every man for himself... just kidding," smiling.

Avionic switches—"OFF."

Fuel Shutoff—"PUSHED IN."

Key—"IN and BOTH selected."

Friction controls—"loosened and check freedom of controls moving cyclic and collective checking for restriction and/or bindings," as he moved the controls, then returning friction back on.

Carb heater handle—"UP," (handle in up position).

Radios—"OFF."

Strobe—"ON."

Ignition switch— set to "BOTH."

Engine priming—set to "START." He twisted the throttle on the collective a few times and set for start.

Check area" Clear left" he called out looking over his shoulder. I responded, "Clear right."

Starter button. "PRESS," to Start.

He pressed it on the collective and the Lycoming VO 435 began coming to life. The rpm gauge began to climb to 1600 then 1700 rpm. As it rose, Sam pointed to the oil pressure gauge and the rotor rpm increasing suggesting a normal start. The rotor blades were turning and the machine began rocking gently and growing louder. Sam pointed to the oil temp and cylinder gauges coming up and in the green and gave me a thumbs-up. The radios were turned on as he listened to the weather report.

"Okay, let's do the last checks and then we're ready to go, what we call the mag checks." The rpm slowly began to increase to 3000 rpm and he checked the drop in rpm as each mag was selected on the panel. He adjusted the throttle and the rotor rpm for flight.

"Take off checklist." We ran through the items on the checklist.

"Take off check completed," Sam finally called. He looked around the airfield as he spoke into the microphone. "Good morning Tower, Gabriel One Zero requesting takeoff to the South, local VFR."

"Roger, good morning Gabriel One Zero, cleared takeoff present position, winds 040 at 6 knots, report clear."

"Thank you, Rita?"

"Morning Sam…out for a little flying today? Good to hear your voice again."

"Yours too darling. Here with my friend Robert. Gabriel One Zero, cleared for takeoff."

"Boy, you sure are friendly with the locals."

"Always try to be… ready Robert?"

"All set."

I didn't even feel it as Sam gently lifted Gabriel into a hover. And before I knew it, we were accelerating rapidly to a red line 83 knots on the airspeed indicator skimming just 10 feet above the ground. Sam gently pulled back on the stick to 500 feet at 1500 feet per minute gluing my butt to the seat. I watched the aircraft parked below shrink.

Next thing I know, we're rolling into a 55-degree angle of bank left turn with a 20-degree nose down attitude, followed by an accelerating climb and similar turn to the right. I was literally hanging in my harness at that point. I thought to myself if this guy is trying to get my attention—he's got it!

"All …right!" I shouted. Sam was clearly enjoying himself as we headed to the coast.

"Tower, Gabriel One Zero clear to the South, over."

Flying With My Higher Self

"Gabriel One Zero, roger, good day y'all."

Laughing, "Hey Sam, ever think about trying out for the Blue Angels?"

Smiling while focused straight ahead "Flown with them I have, but not as much fun as Gabriel here." His expression took on a happy glow. "There is nothing like the freedom and joy of flying a helicopter—nothing like it. Sure, a jet fighter is fun but you just don't feel it, besides you can do more in the helicopter."

He rolled Gabriel into a tight turn and then with aft cyclic and collective, stopped us in midair at exactly 500 feet. Wow! I thought. This guy can fly this machine.

"Can't do that in a jet."

Lowering the nose, we accelerated to a comfortable cruise speed. Sam adjusted the rotor rpm with the collective as the vibration leveled out. Very nice and smooth, I thought.

"Hey Robert, I have a friend, Jan, who lives a few miles from here. How about we pay her a visit?" No sooner than he finished we were diving for the ground leveling off at 50 feet. "She won't expect us this early."

Up ahead, I could see a small cottage in a large fenced field surrounded by trees. A woman appeared to be putting clothes on a clothesline. Must be Jan. Sure enough, she started waving as we flew over.

Sam put Gabriel into a tight left turn, slowing to 20 knots as he flew low, right over the house waving with his free hand. I could see Jan waving both hands wildly, smiling and jumping up and down. Some of the clothes were flying off the line, caught in the rotor wash. She clearly appreciated who I was beginning to think of as "Cowboy Sam."

"Wonderful woman Robert, the best God has created."

"How long have you known each other?"

"Oh, a few years now, and many lifetimes before."

"I see…many lifetimes!" My mind skipped between watching the instruments and the concept of many lifetimes. I was familiar with past lives and had done a past life regression.

We began a slow climb to 500 feet, leveled off and flew quietly for a few minutes.

"So, Sam, where did you train? Where did you learn to fly like that?"

"Well, I have been flying a long time."

"Yeah, military?"

"Yep."

"Which branch?"

"All of them at one time or another."

I looked at him with an incredulous smile. He sure was evasive. "Okay, I understand that ... I'm rather private myself."

"Hey Robert, want to fly?"

"Sure."

"You have the flight controls."

"I have the controls."

Then I flew Gabriel. It was all coming back to me, especially my scan after so many years…attitude indicator, altimeter, airspeed, vertical velocity indicator. It had been over 20 years since I sat at the controls of a helicopter. It felt wonderful.

"Not bad. I see you haven't lost your touch."

"Thanks." We were silent for a moment.

"Feels good, doesn't it. It's in your blood."

"Yeah."

"If you dreamed about flying helicopters, what does it mean to you?" He asked. I glanced over at him; he was watching the sky.

I had to think for a moment about Sam's question. In fact, I frequently dreamed of my flying days.

"Well, it's the freedom Sam. Yeah, it's the sensation of being free and doing something special and demanding, and, at some level, demonstrating mastery and competence."

Sam was nodding in agreement. "Well said. There's that and more, right. Deep within is a desire to be free of all things that tie us down and flying is one way to do it. We want that escape to know that we are back in control of our lives."

"There is something to that." I glanced again in his direction, but he continued on. "What you haven't realized – that most folks don't realize - is that you're already free, and in control of your life."

"Well, yeah, theoretically at least. It doesn't always feel that way although I know, intellectually, everything is my choice. At least in the beginning."

Sam suggested, "Let's head towards the coast—that Okay?"

"Sounds good."

Sam paused and scanned the sky. We were quiet for a few minutes, then, "So Robert, are you local?"

"Moved down almost four years ago, but we'd been visiting the area off and on for years. I used to live about an hour away, back when I was in the military. You?"

"Well, I'm from out and about as well, but I like it around here. Friendly, winters aren't bad, fishing is good, flying is great. I just finally reached a point where I can please myself for awhile, and right now it's here."

"Much the same boat. My wife and I have finally both retired – well, I retired first. From the military, then from teaching, then had a healing practice for a while. We just reached a spot where we could make a dream come true, live on the water. It's been good."

"So, you have practical experience with creating your own change and keeping your freedom. I can tell that it agrees with you. It's a good feeling."

I remembered a phrase from that Ascension handbook, 'What you visualize you create.' I softly recalled out loud, "What you visualize you create." I spent a lot of time teaching that to my clients back in Virginia."

Sam looked at me, his eyes smiling. "I see that you have been doing your homework."

I smiled back at him.

Sam continued, "Guess people have to experience that for themselves. But, it's true. Whatever you consistently visualize and hold steady in your thoughts will sooner or later materialize."

"The law of attraction."

"That's right."

I'd, of course, read about it, tried to practice it. I began to practice manifesting things in my life. I'd had mixed success I think. Of course, how do you measure success in that sort of thing anyway? But now, here was someone I could talk to about it without being looked at as some kind of wacko.

"Seriously, I've read about it. But how does it work from a practical standpoint?" I asked.

"I have the controls. Let's head back to the barn." I was amazed how time had flown by (ugh, bad pun), and wasn't altogether sure that Sam hadn't blown off my question.

"Tower, Gabriel One Zero 3 miles to the west for landing."

"Roger, Gabriel One Zero, clear to land runway 6 R, hover taxi to parking. Caution air show, aircraft on ramp. Winds 050 degrees at 6 knots."

"Gabriel One Zero, clear to land."

III

What you see in the world reflects a process in your mind,
That starts with the idea of what you wish.
You are your own master.
Whatever you visualize; you create.

As we completed the final post-flight checklist, Sam asked, "Do you have time for a coffee and doughnut or something?" He headed toward the small, empty café at the airfield.

Settling in, Sam leaned forward on the Formica tabletop. "You had asked about manifesting."

"Yes…how it works, practically."

"Let's try something. Close your eyes for a moment, Robert." I'm game, I thought, expecting to recall something from the flight. "Good." Sam said. "Now tell me what you see."

"Nothing…it's like a dark canvas with no form."

I wondered where this was going.

"Right. Keep 'em closed and really pay attention. Imagine… the key is to imagine yourself free of the constraints of time and space and allow yourself to go anywhere. Just play around, think about it and tell me what you experience."

I opened my eyes momentarily, closed them again, concentrated. I could not bring myself into a no time-space realm. Maybe I was trying to hard—a bad habit.

"Sam, I'm not getting it."

"Right… it's sometimes difficult to go there unless you are in a dream or altered meditative state, in other words very relaxed. Hard to stay focused, right?"

"Right."

"This just takes some practice. Just relax and think about what you want to create."

I took some deep breaths to relax and tried to picture myself on a beautiful beach somewhere. All I really pictured was myself sitting like a fool in the airport restaurant.

"What do you see?"

"Same thing, just darkness and a little form and some sparkles of light, otherwise darkness."

"Okay, try this. Keep your eyes closed and imagine you are flying. Just think of flying without constraints of the physical world. What do you see now?"

I chuckled.

"Yes, I am flying, but…I am all over the place. I am flying over places—really fast."

"Any place in particular?"

"Started in LA and was over New Delhi moving faster than I thought possible. Right now, I am orbiting the earth like a spaceship."

"Good, how did you do that?"

"I focused, just relaxed and imagined myself doing it, like a kid pretending."

Sam laughed. "Excellent. You pictured something that did not exist in your physical, sensing reality and you experienced this. Think another flying thought."

"I am with my mother in California now seeing her in her garden, actually hovering over her home …"

"Right. Ever had a dream where you were flying over a city, town or your own bedroom?"

I opened my eyes. "Yes, I have."

"You see, you imagined it and it became your reality. The imagination is a very powerful energy. What you imagine you create. Or, more precisely, co-create."

"So, like creating something with your eyes and hands; you first imagine what you wish to create."

"Precisely. That's how I got to fly helicopters. By visualizing. My thoughts triggered the reality flying the Bell 47, but my training has been in co-creating and manifesting my imagination in many other ways. I imagine something and the thought becomes a word, which then becomes an action or experience. I create it as my reality. There are many ways to fly, Robert. It's your choice. Right now, I am loving this Bell 47."

"So, by just thinking of something…or imagining, I am co-creating a potential reality."

"That's right. At some level, you have manifested the experience. Through the power of your own imagination you aligned yourself with your creative power. If you trace all the thoughts you had beforehand going back, you would find that there were some synchronicities and events that led you to flying with me today. You just followed them, like breadcrumbs."

I paused for a moment to take this all in. "Just like my house on the water. I imagined it and it happened."

"Yes. The Universal Mind creates whatever you think about. Remember this: The universe always says YES. At a deep level, you know this. You can create any reality you want; there are no limits to what you can have. Most people just don't remember that they can create their own reality."

I stepped into it a little further. "I've studied a lot of energy healing modalities – and believe that the imagination has a frequency—a vibratory energy that creates our world through our thoughts and beliefs."

"I agree, Robert. As you say, these are powerful energies that manifest and we've got to keep the enormous power of imagination on the right frequency. Hold positive thoughts and you will manifest and see a positive world. You envision good unfolding in every area of your life. The opposite is also true. Holding negativity manifests that."

I added, "Like if I am afraid of something and spend time thinking about some bad outcome ... that unwanted thing may become a reality. The Universe gives you what you ask for. I used to tell my clients that we create from an inner state of being, in what seems to be outside ourselves. It can be either good, bad or neutral just a matter of deciding and choosing what you want to see in your life."

Sam had folded his arms, leaned back, and looked around the cafe. "The creator is not passive in this process. He did not give a manual for failure. There are no victims here. You reap what you sow. Create a positive experience and you'll have positive results. The reverse is true, as well. We've both seen it.

"Hey, slightly different subject, Robert. What's the fastest speed you can imagine?"

"Light...186,000 feet per second, I think."

"Right. Your thoughts travel even faster. Ponder that little concept. If I want to travel to Jupiter, all I have to do is think about it and I'm there. It's called thought projection. Try it sometime."

I shook my head and laughed. "Hey, how about we both imagine that we're flying again at 0900 tomorrow?"

Sam chortled, "Sounds good, see you then cowboy, and... good job today!"

That evening at home, I flipped through the handbook and landed on a page that read:

You can create any reality you want; In the imagined Universe, all is possible. Even the Universe, beautiful, perfect and loving.

IV

*Spirituality doesn't mean going somewhere
else or someplace better;
it means learning to live in balance where you are now.
It is connecting with Spirit within and throughout YOU.*

I rounded the aircraft and saw him standing by Gabriel, enjoying the cool of the day. I had brought the Ascension Handbook with me, just in case we had a few minutes to talk about it.

"Morning Sam, brought you some breakfast." I said as I handed him a bag with an Egg McMuffin and some hot coffee.

"Good morning to you sir and thank you. You read my mind. Not sure where one gets breakfast around here with the café closed. Sleep well?"

"Okay. A bit restless. How about you?"

"Well…fine, considering it was my sleeping bag under Gabriel last night. Town was all sold out with the air show."

"You should have said something; I have an empty guest room all ready, Sam."

"Thanks, and nice of you to offer. I like my time alone sometimes, I am sure you understand."

Actually, I did.

Sam had set up two reclining chairs by Gabriel; we slid into them.

Fumbling with the lid on the coffee, I said, "Hey Sam, you were in a dream I had last night."

"Oh...you remember it? What was it about?"

"Us. You and me flying 47's. I had mine and you were in Gabriel. We were flying in formation."

"Who was flight lead?" he asked with a sly grin.

"Funny you ask. We were flying side by side. I noticed because that's a little unusual." Finally got the lid off without spilling.

"How'd it feel?" he asked.

"Well, it was strange. It was as if we were headed on a mission—with a strong sense of purpose— but we didn't need radios because our thoughts were synchronized."

"Where to?"

"Don't know. Then something strange happened – well, like it happens in dreams."

"I am in suspense!" he said, chewing the sandwich.

"You were gone and I was left flying alone."

"I just disappeared?"

"Just like that."

"Whoa. I see. How'd that *feel* to you?"

"Well, odd...like I'd lost a really good friend."

"I'm flattered that you'd think that. You felt as if I had left you?"

"Yes, in a way. But I wasn't worried, or angry. I could handle whatever came next. I remembered the whole thing completely, not just bits and fragments. The weird thing was that, when I woke up I felt at peace, as if I had accepted everything somehow. Not sure why I felt that way."

Sam looked at me patiently. "What was your take-away?"

"That peaceful feeling; gave me a reassurance that all is well."

"Always is. There is divine perfection in everything. All is in Divine order, my friend." We just sat, each absorbed in our own thoughts.

I remembered reading in the handbook, *Don't be dismayed by goodbyes. A farewell is necessary before you can meet again. And meeting again, after moments or lifetimes is certain for those who are friends...*

"Do you believe it?" He said suddenly.

"Believe what?"

"That there are no goodbyes."

Sam paused, looked out as a small trainer lifted off the end of the runway. I quietly said,

"I guess, I think friends are always together, inseparable, and you have memories."

He paused, then said, "No, what I mean is that we really don't die…life never ends you see. It continues – you just change form. Don't need to say goodbye all the time."

"Are you saying that death as we know it, or as popular culture portrays it, does not exist?"

"Yeah, that's right. Think of how many times you have *died* in this lifetime, Robert."

I paused but Sam went on, "Need a little help?"

"Let's see…your first marriage, changes, moves, different careers, evolving beliefs, shifting values and perceptions, these and many more have been *deaths* in a way of life that no longer served you on the path. You call them transitions, but they are really small deaths. It's a good thing. They were necessary experiences for your growth."

He laughed. "Hey Robert, you know there is the good and the bad news about death…dying."

"I can't wait to hear this."

"The bad news is you are going to die."

"And what's the good news?"

"The good news is that you are going to die."

"So, dying to our life as we know it is good and bad. What a concept Sam."

"That's right. Death as you know it happens all the time, and it's called change, evolution and moving forward in life."

Had I mentioned my first marriage? Not for the first time, I wondered just who he was. I fell silent thinking about the dream.

Sam went on, "The act of dreaming was a death experience. At death, the soul leaves the body and travels into the astral realms of the higher dimensions.

It so happened that you chose to fly with me. Later, your soul traveled back into the body."

"So, what you are saying is that we die every day unconsciously?"

"Right, a death of a sort. Look at it this way. In your dream, there was the illusion of my disappearing when in reality you wanted to experience something new—let's call it solo flight for the sake of simplicity. Do you see where I am going here?"

"Sort of…How do you know all this; where did you learn it?"

"Let's just say I have been practicing for a while."

This was so much more than I expected. I picked up the handbook and, flipping through. This is what I found:

Take your dying less seriously. When you remember where you came from and why you are here, death is but a coming home.

I set it aside. Dying seemed a long way off.

Sam sat up "Hey, let's try something. Just relax. Get comfortable, close your eyes and take a few deep breaths."

I did as Sam asked and closed my eyes.

"Good, now, He instructed. Listen carefully. I want you to go back into the dream that you had last night. Take your time. Try to remember all the details. I will do my best to dream the dream with you and we can compare experiences afterwards."

I closed my eyes and began slow breathing. Soon, I felt myself going back in the dream, floating into space, effortlessly, going higher and higher. Then, I was flying the 47 again, yet I was by myself flying above the clouds. I looked around to see if I could find Sam and he suddenly showed up flying on my left side just like in the dream last night. And then when I looked again he was gone. But when I turned to look over my right shoulder there he was again. When I looked up he was above me and then below me ahead about a mile. Then he was gone.

I don't know how long I sat there; but, after a while, I slowly came back into the here and now. Sam was nowhere to be seen. I had to find him.

You are always free to change your mind and choose a different future, or a different past..

V

Your only obligation in a lifetime is to be true to yourself.

The four-day air show was winding down and the crowds were growing smaller.

I wondered if Sam would be leaving, too. Later, I would measure our time together not by the number of flights we had, but by our talks and how I was changed afterwards.

As we sat at the café watching the afternoon scene on the tarmac, I asked, "Sam, do you normally talk to your students liked we've talked?"

"No. You're the exception, Robert."

"Well…I've enjoyed it. Don't understand everything yet, but that's part of a deeper understanding of life. You've made it make sense, seem so easy, this imagining stuff, creating and manifesting your own reality, to use your words."

He looked up from the table and stared at me as he bit into his hotdog. "Well, the world is your imagination Robert. You are the magician of your life, and don't even know it."

"Meaning?"

"That your thoughts are the creative force that manifests. Right?"

I nodded. "Well, I can imagine wanting many things in my life now, but I don't see them actualized."

He raised his eyebrows. "Really. I'd dispute that."

"Okay, you're right, I've been very fortunate to have gotten almost everything I've wanted in some fashion. And I am grateful. It's just not in the way you describe it."

"Remember, to bring anything into your life, you have to imagine it as if it is already there."

"Give me an example, please."

"Okay, let's do an experiment. Start small, at first. Imagine anything you want to manifest now."

I looked around and saw the swallow's nest tucked under the corner of the hangar roof. "I love birds... A white feather."

White Feather

I closed my eyes and fixed the image in my mind, the whole feather bathed in a golden light. "Okay, done, I can see it."

"Open your eyes now, Robert."

"Where's my feather?"

"Did you have it clear in your mind?'

"Yes."

"Did you believe that you already had it?"

"Yes, I did."

"Then wait for it to manifest and trust that it will."

"That's it?"

"That's it." Sam said.

Throughout the day, I looked for my feather, believing that it would show up, but nothing showed up. That afternoon, after lunch, I asked, "Seriously, where did you learn all this stuff, Sam; all this metaphysical talk—you know —dreams, death, manifesting?"

"Interesting you'd ask. You see, we all share this knowledge. I just chose to remember it."

"You lost me, again."

"Well, this is your first flying lesson—let's call it ground school for the sake of simplicity. You have a basic understanding of helicopter aerodynamics—right?"

"Why...yeah."

"Yet it's been over 20 plus years since you last flew in one, other than Gabriel. Right?"

"Yeah, how did you know? I'm sure I haven't mentioned it."

He just smiled, ignoring my question. I was beginning to find that a tad irritating. "So, you know how a helicopter works. If I were to ask you some questions to jog your memory you could probably find the right answers."

"Maybe …. probably."

"What was the max range of the Sikorsky MH-53J PAVELOW with 9,000 pound cargo load?"

I thought for a moment, "About 285 nautical miles, unrefueled."

"More like 300 at cruise speed of 105 knots, right?"

"Right. how did you…? Okay, where are you going with this?"

"You chose to remember what you already knew. The knowledge was there, tucked away in your memory—the hard drive of the brain."

I pondered this for a moment.

Sam continued, "Have you ever felt as if you have been on this planet before? That some of your experiences felt familiar, perhaps, sometimes learning flowed naturally as if you had done the problems before."

"Oh yeah. Sort of déjà vu. I've had situations where I have met people for the first time and had a strong sense of familiarity as if I knew them, but not knowing why or where. I think it's pretty common."

I paused for a moment, "What you're saying is that I already know what I need to know and that all I have to do is remember. That's it."

"Precisely. I couldn't have said it any better. When you came to this planet from Spirit you knew everything, conceptually that is. You had the knowledge of who you are as pure spirit created in the image and essence of the All-That-Is-God. There was nothing you needed to know or learn. That is who you are and always will be. You chose to experience yourself in the physicality of the earth plane going from infinite consciousness to finite consciousness and in this process you forgot who you really are. In other words, your job on earth is not to learn but to remember who you are. This is your soul's purpose."

I thought of all the times I had struggled, prayed, and searched for my purpose. I'd always felt that if I could just latch on to a greater purpose my life would be more rewarding, satisfying somehow. Just remembering, that's it?

I shook my head. "It seems so self-defeating to have to forget everything to remember it again."

Sam chuckled. "Well, you signed up to play the game of life, of experiencing the good and bad of the University of Earth. The main premise of this game was that you were to forget, I call it a mild case of amnesia. You were gifted with that to ensure maximum evolution and growth."

"But you said that we all share this knowledge."

"Yes, we are One in the image and likeness of the Creator, yet different in the expressions of who we are. We may be physically different, but our *essence* is the same—and we all have the ability to create and know ourselves as Sons and Daughters of God. It's about knowing that we're enough, good enough, just as we are."

Suddenly we got quiet, both staring at the distance, as these thoughts began to sink in.

"I know, it's a hard concept to wrap yourself around."

"Yes, but I keep going back to why I chose to forget who I was? Why on earth would I do that?"

"To know yourself experientially. It is God experiencing himself through you. That's what the Creator wanted and how the game is played. It's the only way to allow your true Self to be *Who You Are* rather that just know yourself conceptually as a part of Spirit. Everyone's task here on earth is to return to God by remembering that we are part of God. We do this by co-creating and experiencing all aspects of ourselves as a part of the essence of *Who We Are*."

"This is the divine plan; to express the God potential within us?"

"Yep."

"Where is the illusion then, I mean we hear that we are living in an illusory world?"

"The illusion is that you are separate from Source energy, that you are something other than Spirit. Your soul knows the truth, but you, as a physical being here, you simply choose not to access certain files or memories."

I noticed the hangar shadow was almost to our chairs. "Hey Sam, if we're flying this afternoon, we need to get going."

"Right, want to start the flight plan?" We both jumped up and headed for the hangar.

Driving home that evening, I noticed a flock of seagulls overhead. As I pulled into the driveway and got out of the car, I noticed the white feather lying on the pavement. I bent over and picked it up smiling. Later, I opened the handbook and read:

We are not learning anything, we are merely remembering what we already know. Just be who you are; calm, clear and bright, and you will attract those who need to learn from you and from whom you will learn from.

VI

*Listen carefully to the inner desires of
your heart—your conscience.
We are all learners and doers.
Humor dissolves all barriers.
Laugh more!*

"Hey Robert, let's go fly. It's a glorious day!" He practically bounced out of Gabriel as I turned the corner.

"You're in a good mood today, Sam." I commented.

"Try to be all the time. Life is too short not to be happy, if you get my drift."

In fact, it was a beautiful morning--a blue, cloudless sky and slight breeze from the West. The not-too-warm moist air felt very comfortable. We did a preflight and completed the pre-start and start checklists. Sam lifted Gabriel into a hover and taxied to the edge of the ramp adjacent to a large white-lined field. *Must be soccer, the goal nets were lined up by the fence.*

"Okay, Robert, today, we're going to start with some basic hover work so you get a good feel for Gabriel here. She has a nice feel in the controls, some dampening but overall good, basic stick and rudder response."

"No AFCS?"

"Nope, we don't have the automatic flight control system here so it takes some getting used to. In fact, you fly this aircraft and you'll find others easy. Makes you a better pilot. Of course, you already know that, right?"

I just nodded.

"We'll do a constant heading square at five feet altitude. Watch me."

Sam guided the helicopter to one of the white lines to his left. "The constant-heading square is a maneuver done at a constant heading with reference to an object outside the cockpit, in this case we're working off the white lines there. I'm going to place the center of the helicopter over the line."

Sam expertly glided Gabriel forward with the cyclic and with a slight collective adjustment stayed on the line, stopping at the corner. He then applied a little right cyclic, placing the tip of the skids over one side of the square. Once we reached the corner of the square he stopped and began to back up. It was fun doing this in the H-53 with 99 feet of fuselage behind the pilot.

"I get in the habit of adding a little power as I bring aft cyclic in since the tail has a tendency to dip in the rotor stream. And watch the wind direction. Questions?"

"No. Got it."

"Good, you have the flight controls."

"I have the controls."

I moved them gently. It took just a moment to realize how responsive they were and how I was over-controlling. The helicopter moved awkwardly from side to side like it was being slapped around.

Sam just laughed. "Glad we got a box big enough to do this in..."

"Hey, I don't need that kind of encouragement." I barked back. Sam laughed again.

It brought back memories years ago of my first flight learning to hover the Navy Bell TH-57 helicopter. I was all over the place and to make matters worse, the Navy tower controller chimed in asking if I needed any assistance! Go figure. I thought that guy probably did it to all the students on their first flight just to rattle them.

Slowly, I began to get the feel for the 47 and flew the box trying not to over-control from fear, but just relaxing, taking a deep breath, and resting my right arm on my knee, using small wrist movements and collective as needed.

"Gabriel's quite sensitive," I observed. "Right, no trim," I said concentrating.

Flying With My Higher Self

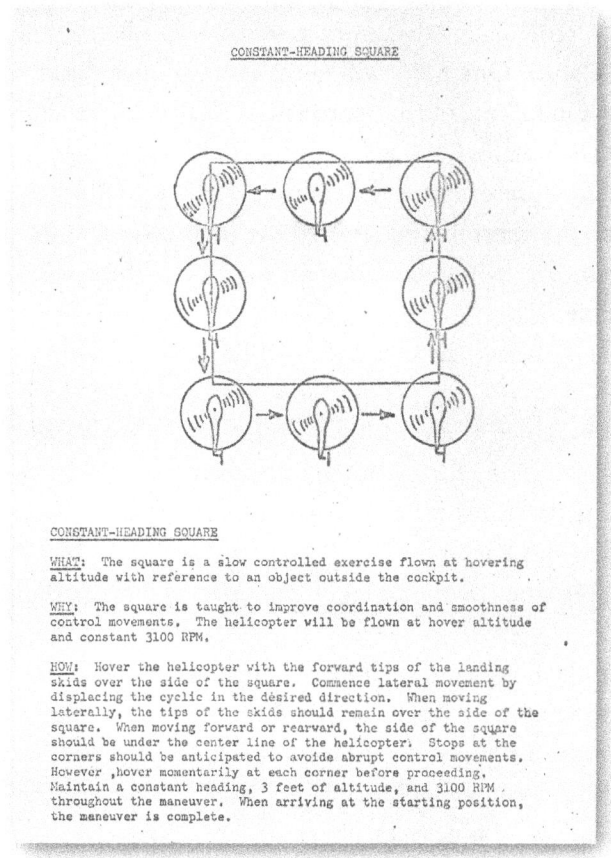

Constant-heading Square

Sam didn't let my dogged effort shut him up. "Back when Bell designed the 47, there was no need for an electrical trim system like the one you're used to. As the helicopters got bigger and heavier they needed it. The new digital fly-by-wire systems have no trim. Their all electrical now. Nice job, Robert. Now, let's try it the other way."

Suddenly the radio transmission cut in. "Gabriel One Zero, Tower."

Sam quickly responded "Tower, Gabriel One Zero, go ahead, over."

"Gabriel One Zero, just received a distress call from Aero Piper transiting eastbound with in-flight emergency. Lost contact several minutes ago. Have alerted local authorities. Can you check it out?"

"Roger…do you have approximate position, over?"

"Roger, approximately five miles to southwest… best guess, One Zero."

"Roger, Gabriel One Zero, will check it out. Request takeoff clearance."

"Gabriel One Zero, much appreciated, cleared for takeoff present position, winds 230/4 knots."

"Gabriel One Zero. I have the controls, Robert."

Sam took the controls and lowered the nose as we made a fast beeline to the Southwest. He looked determined, focused. There was somebody out there in trouble.

I thought unexpectedly of Chuck and P.T. always looking for opportunities to help.

I intently scanned ahead trying to pick out anything unusual.

We had been flying for about ten minutes when I saw it. "Sam, looks like some smoke at 10 o'clock for about two miles. See it?"

"Yeah, let's check it out."

As we approached, Sam brought Gabriel down to the treetops. We circled the area.

"Come right a bit. Sam, we have wreckage down there! Looks like a small plane on fire. I can barely make it all out through the smoke."

Sam was already adjusting the rotor speed and power, slowing Gabriel as we flew over the crash site looking for a place to land. The area was covered in dense brush and large pine trees.

"Not many places to land here."

"Sam, what do you think, should we let somebody know we've found it."

"Right." We began a slow climb. "Tower, Gabriel One Zero" I called on the radio.

"Gabriel… One Zero… tower, you… coming in garbled… say again…"

"Roger, Gabriel One Zero, over a crash site 11 miles west of location in dense brush…will remain on site to render any assistance."

"Copy… Gabr …. crash site…."

"Gabriel One Zero, out."

Sam eased Gabriel back down to the treetops.

"Sam…this area looks very isolated. It'll be pretty tough for rescue folks to get out here. Winds look like they are light and variable."

Flying With My Higher Self

"Robert, is that a small opening in the tree line directly off the nose?" Sam began his approach.

"Looks pretty tight," I interjected.

We hovered directly over the trees. I looked down and back behind us. There were large pine trees all around and below them were smaller trees. Making a landing impossible.

I chimed, "There's an opening to our right, about 300 feet. Looks as if the plane cleared a path through the trees…we may be able to land there."

"Okay," a tense Sam responded.

Sam pedal turned and shot his approach to a small clearing amongst a cluster of downed trees adjacent to a charred section of the brush. He gently set Gabriel down while trying to avoid the tree stumps, sloped terrain, and shutdown. "Let's go!" he said. I grabbed the first aid kit.

We loped through the charred brush still smoldering with the smell of aviation gasoline. The tail section and a large part of the right wing were visible among the chopped trees as we neared the site. I thought the pilot did a heck of a job just keeping the aircraft level as he sliced through the trees. We quickly scanned the wreckage.

"Sam over here." I pointed and started running again.

About 100 feet from the burning fuselage was an elderly man lying on his back. His hands were badly burned. His face was scratched and bleeding a little, but otherwise he looked alive. He must have pulled himself out and crawled from the burning aircraft or was thrown on impact. Maybe both. I flipped open the kit and started pulling out gauze and antibiotic ointment.

"Robert, you stay with him and I will check for anyone else."

"Sir, you are going to be alright," I said to him.

"Are you the pilot?" He nodded slowly with just one eye open, then patted my hand and whispered, "Alone," telling me he was the only occupant. He mumbled softly "power… loss."

I acknowledged it. "Don't worry sir…helps on the way," I said reassuringly.

I saw Sam inspecting the wreckage trying to see if anyone else was in it, but the fire prevented him from getting closer. I shouted, "Sam, he was alone." Don't know if he heard me.

I took off my jacket and placed it over him, then checked for broken bones and any bleeding, puncture wounds. The poor guy just looked dazed, in shock, shivering. He needed help right away. My energy medicine training kicked in and I placed my hand over his heart and sacrum and gently sent loving energy to his energy field trying to relax him as much as possible till help arrived. I did a natural body working technique, smoothing out his energy field, balancing the energy centers while gently reassuring him. He was still shaking a little but slowly began to relax. His breath began to slow down and he closed his eyes.

Sam walked up to me shaking his head. "Couldn't see anyone else. Robert. You stay with him…I'll see about getting some help. The authorities will have a hell of a time getting to this location through this smoke and stuff," Sam gasped as he gestured broadly around the area.

Sam walked back to Gabriel then trotted back to give me a couple of water bottles. A few minutes later, he flew off. I sat with the old man; he seemed quiet but not asleep or unconscious.

It wasn't long before Sam was back. Behind him, an Emergency Medical Technician with a small bag jumped out of the aircraft. His shirt read "Ralph." He immediately knelt next to the injured pilot and began checking the vitals and radioing information back.

For the next hour, Sam flew back and forth to the crash site, stopping to refuel and ferrying personnel and law enforcement. Eventually, a better landing site was cleared and the medical helicopter was able to come in with emergency personnel. Police, local rescue, and I contrived a makeshift path to ease egress and helped put out the fires.

That evening, Sam and I sat in the airport cafe in silence. He looked at me, smiled and said, "You did some nice work today Robert. Acted like you had done this before."

"We were lucky. Glad to be able to help. That was some great flying Sam…"

"Tough patch of ground to go down in."

The waitress brought our sandwiches and looked at us both smiling. "My manager says this is on the house…you guys deserve it after what you all did today. It's all over the news. You got there just in time. Looks like the pilot is going to make it. His family is with him now. It's a miracle!" She paused, "Holler if you want anything else. Glad you were here today."

Rita, the tower controller came over to say hello and congratulate us on a job well done.

"You boys did a great job today. Y'all come up and visit me some time, over coffee and tell me the whole story, Okay?"

My mind went back to moments before: *Act like you've done this before. Act like you've done this before...*

20 April, 1996

"Cowboy 20, Albuquerque Center."

"Center, Cowboy 20, go ahead sir."

"Cowboy 20, your Command Post has requested immediate return to base, contact them on 124.6 when able."

We were twenty miles southwest of the Air Force base in a military training area working with a Special Forces (SOF) team and had been flying for over 3.5 hours.

"Roger, Center. Request clearance present position."

The Sikorsky MH-53J Pave Low helicopter climbed.

"Cowboy 20, Albuquerque Center...turn right 350 and climb to 1500 feet, squawk 3428 and contact tower 315.8. Good day."

"Cowboy 20, right to 350, out of 300 feet to 1500, squawking 3428."

"Cowboy 20, Command Post."

"Cowboy 20. Go ahead.

"Roger, Cowboy 20, we have priority request from the Air Force Rescue Coordination Center about a lost hiker with life threatening injuries in the Gila National Forest approximately 180 miles southwest requiring immediate evacuation. We do not have contact with them. No civilian air assets are available. Can you assist? Have approximate coordinates, over?"

"Roger, ready to copy."

We plotted the location on the map and entered them in the Central Avionics Computer (CAC), Elevation 8300 feet/Temp 77 degrees.

"Roger, command post, request ground refueling and we have special forces medic onboard. Need paramedic-rescue. Also, any tanker assets available?"

"Roger, team will meet you at the aircraft. Will check on tankers."

After topping of our tanks and dropping off the A-team (the SOF medic volunteered to come along), we picked up our passengers, loaded the 42,000 pound MH-53J helicopter and departed.

Two hours later, as darkness set in, we arrived at the hiker's location. We flew right over the area and set up a search pattern while computing power, bingo fuel and completing the landing checklist and hover coupler for automatic approach and hover. We figured we had computed just enough fuel for 20-minute loiter, hoist and enough fuel to get us home.

"Coming right, scanners let me know if you see anything."

"Cowboy 20, Command Post."

"Command Post, Cowboy 20…"

"Cowboy 20, we are working to get a tanker for you."

"Roger, CP, thank you."

MH-53 Pave Low Doing Hoist Recovery

The MH-53J is over 99 feet long with three scanners on the left, right and tail; they are also aerial gunners on special operations missions. After about five minutes circling we heard, "Right scanner to pilot."

"Pilot."

"Sir, I believe I see movement below, one o'clock quarter mile."

"Roger, coming right for flyover."

The flight engineer adjusted the forward-looking infrared (FLIR) to the area.

"Call the mark."

"Come right five degrees sir, looking good, straight ahead now 300 meters."

We flew over the spot and, sure enough, it was our hiker with two other men, one waving his hat frantically. The engineer entered the new coordinates into the CAC.

"Steering please, coming around, confirm checklist complete."

"Roger sir, gear down, throttles coming up." The rpm increased to the maximum 105 percent on the rotor tachometer.

"Engineer, what is my power?"

"Sir, 90 percent available, 85 required OGE (out of ground effect), Pressure altitude 8354 feet."

"Scanners report."

"Sir, right scanner…looks real tight, tall trees all around, may be at max height for hoist; final heading looks good."

"Sir, left scanner, looks real tight, will have large trees on left side."

"Tail agrees. No maneuver room, sir."

"Flight Engineer—will have to hover above trees, sir and drop hoist."

"Okay guys, we'll be shooting this approach and checking power on final and then come around for the pickup."

"Copilot, back me up on the hover coupler…"

"Copilot, Roger."

"Copy left, right, tail."

"On final approach," as I began slowing the MH-53J descending at 100 feet per minute.

The engineer called the groundspeed on the forward looking infrared digital display: 80… 70… 60… 50… 40… 30…,

"Okay, power looks good…used 80 percent, coming around again for hoist pick-up."

"Engineer to pilot, we have fifteen minutes fuel to Bingo."

You are going to make it!

"Scanners, report."

"Roger, this is it… turning to final."

We came around to final approach and it was dark, so I was flying on night vision goggles and on instruments.

"Charlie, stay with me on the controls and be ready to engage the coupler, in case."

"Roger."

"Engineer, notify medic and P.J.'s we are on final."

"Airspeed 60…50…cleared down left, right and tail."

"Stop down, watch descent…"

"Altitude good, 200 meters off the nose, keep slowing sir."

You are coming in too fast, slow it down…"

"Slow it, sir!" came crying over the intercom. We flew past them. I leveled the aircraft,

"Come back 25 meters, watch the trees."

"Stop back."

"Power—95%... RPM Okay… left 10."

The engineer had his hands on the overhead throttles. "Stop down, watch the tail… back."

"Survivor below."

"Hold… looking good."

"Hold. Good hover."

"Hoist going down."

"Hold. Good hover."

There were no visual references as we held the hover over the trees for what seemed like an eternity. The medic and PJ's went down to assist the hiker. Minutes passed.

"Hold. Good hover."

"Sir, we are at Bingo."

"Roger, PJ's going down the hoist."

"On the ground."

"Okay let's get these guys up fast…"

Minutes go by. "Hiker coming up." Minutes later, "Last man in the door. Everyone's in."

"Roger, takeoff checklist…coming out, steering to air refueling control point. 341.6 please."

Flying With My Higher Self

"Cleared forward left, right, tail…"
"After takeoff checklist complete."
"Not bad!"
I remember that voice well.

The injured hiker recovered. Doctors credited his recovery to our quick actions. He had a compound fracture and broken back from a fall; lots of blood loss and would have died had we not got him out when we did. On our return leg, we conducted a night vision goggle aerial refueling from an HC-130 Combat Shadow aircraft. Total flight time 9.5 hours. It had been a long day.

If you do good to even one of my children, you are doing good to me.
If you can save one life during your lifespan, you have achieved something.
Act like you've done this before…

"Where did this come from," I wondered. Sam was watching me closely then turned to study the sandwich he was ripping into.

"That was close, wasn't it?"

"Yeah, we sure helped this guy today…"

"No, I was referring to the hiker…"

Now incredulous, "How did you know?"

He smiled. "Do you remember the words you told yourself during the flight to the hiker's position?"

"No. What words?"

"Lord, help me to get there safely and on time…and get this guy!"

"And the voice talking you through the approach."

"The engineer, scanners…"

"No…the other one…in your head and heart."

"Vaguely. What are you trying to say, Sam?" I was tired, without warning I was just plain exhausted.

"That thought or intention went out and was answered. You co-created the experience or opportunity and it was honored. Your aircraft and aircrew were all instruments to make this reality for you. You are not without help. If you ask sincerely it will be answered. You are getting guidance every minute of the day from your higher self. That still voice that knows where to turn, which path to take, which answers to give, which action to take, which reality to create if you truly seek communion and unity with it."

"Did not Jesus say, *"I am with you, even unto the end of time. The key is to listen and trust."*

From within I heard, *"You are needed, your courage is needed, your faith is needed, your willingness to connect with spirit is needed. You have been blessed with a sense of purpose."*

I am deeply grateful, on my journey, for the parenting and guidance of my higher self. Suddenly talking like that with Sam didn't seem odd anymore.

VII

You are a beam of living love-light,
Waiting to pour forth
From your mind and heart and spirit.
My light shines in you!

The next day was clear and after taking care of a couple of small maintenance issues, Sam gave me a mischievous look saying, "Are you ready to practice auto-rotations?"

It had been awhile since I done one; years, to be exact. Never felt comfortable doing them. "May as well, can't dance."

All helicopter pilots must be able to execute a flawless autorotation. It's an emergency procedure usually done right after an engine failure in a single engine helicopter. The engine powers the main transmission transmitting the power (torque) to the main and tail rotor during flight. If an engine quits the freewheeling mechanism automatically uncouples the engine input to the transmission so that the rotor blades can rotate freely. Helicopter pilots practice the maneuver often because they know that they may have to perform it unexpectedly. You only get one try. Do it wrong and you risk serious injury and possible death. *If you walk away, you did a good job*, as they say.

To practice the maneuver, the pilot reduces the engine power simulating uncoupling and total loss of power. Then, the pilot *immediately* lowers the collective (power lever) to adjust the pitch of the blades, finds the best glide airspeed and a suitable area to land. Frankly, the thought of gliding a powerless helicopter is always unwelcome.

Sam flew Gabriel to 1000 feet above the ground.

"Okay, Robert, I'll demo one for you. If you want you can ride the controls with me. This is a little different than what you were used to. You'll see."

A wide-open farmer's field loomed ahead.

"Here we go." Sam lowered the collective while rolling the throttle to idle. The rotor and engine tachometers registered a split while he adjusted the speed to 60 knots on the airspeed indicator. The vertical velocity indicator registered 1500-1700 feet per minute rate of decent. In other words, we were dropping like a rock.

We quickly arrived at 75 feet where he flared, pulling back on the cyclic to slow the rate of descent and airspeed. At 20 feet we had about 20 knots groundspeed. He gently lowered the nose to the landing attitude at 10 feet, with 5-10 knots groundspeed while pulling full up the collective to soften the landing. Once on the ground he lowered the collective while adjusting the cyclic position slightly forward of neutral, then added throttle to return to 3100 rpm. I was impressed.

We slowly lifted and transitioned to forward flight. A few minutes later we reached the practice altitude, and as we lined up on the field, Sam turned to me. "Questions?"

"Not right away..."

"Ready to try?"

"Yeah."

"As you lower the collective, you may need a little aft cycle. Okay, you have the controls."

"I have the controls."

I climbed to 1000 feet and turned to line up on the field. I lowered the collective as Sam rolled the power off, and before I knew it we were in a rapid descent.

And just then it all appeared like magic—like I had practiced thousands of times as the Sikorsky MH-53 autorotation emergency procedure flashed in my mind.

Flying With My Higher Self

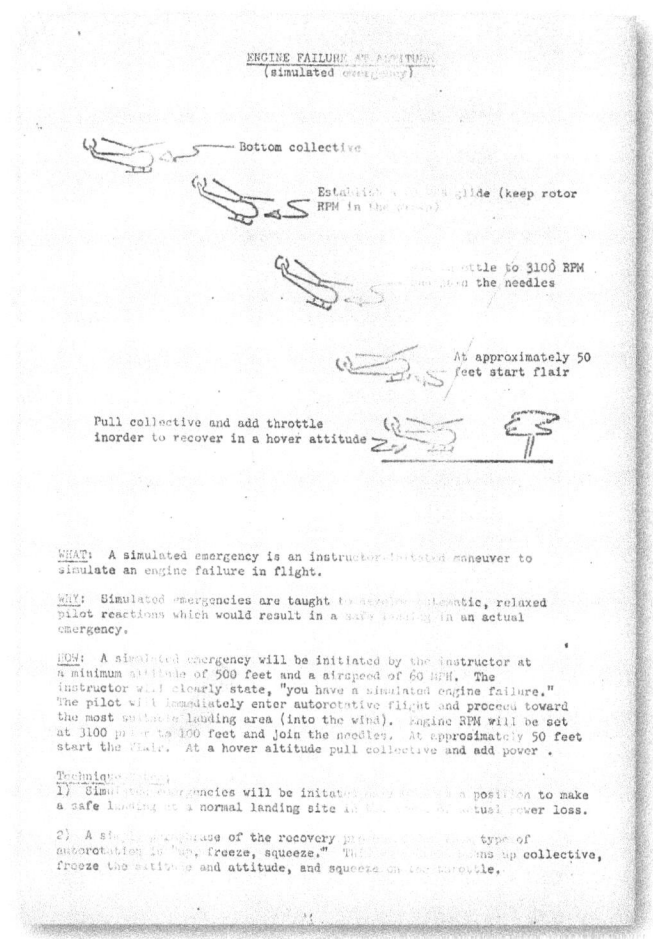

Straight-in Autorotation to Hover

AUTOROTATION--ENTER IMMEDIATELY
COLECTIVE-- FULL DOWN
AIRSPEED--100 KNOTS
GEAR--DOWN
FLARE AT 250 above ground level
AT 50 FT LEVEL THE NOSE (NO HIGHER THAN 10 DEGREES TO AVOID TAIL STRIKE)
AT 10 FT PULL UP COLLECTIVE TO CUSHION LANDING

Upon entry, the nose dipped down a little as I added aft cyclic to get 60 knots.

Here we go—there's the split...coming up on 100 feet, aft cyclic...flare early—in descent to get 75 feet, speed slowing—50...40...30...still descending and coming up on 20 feet...20 knots, level the nose a bit....10 feet, pull collective 5...4...3...2...1. touchdown. That wasn't so bad!

"Nice job, how did that feel for you?" Sam asked, as he took the controls and began a gradual climb. "You know what I like about autos, Robert?"

"No...what?"

"When you do them it's a feeling of coming alive. Like this is it."

"Like what?"

"Well you know ...here you are flying along nice and happy and all of sudden, you are in a controlled freefall, like being on a rollercoaster on the downhill."

"So, this is ...fun." I felt good, confident, it had all come back as second nature.

"Absolutely. It's a metaphor for life."

I thought, *I can't wait to hear this one!*

Sam looked around, feeling good himself and grinning. "Well, there you are, living your life and things are going well for you when all of a sudden you face a test in the form of a crisis, something unexpected that shakes you, and takes you out of your comfort zone, in our case a complete power loss."

"You find yourself reacting to the crisis?"

"That's right."

"Not sure I'm following this analogy, Sam."

"Bear with me, Okay. Let me demonstrate a 180 degree auto."

Sam entered the 180-degree autorotation downwind as we rolled into a 30-degree angle of bank turn for the field. As we descended, he continued, "First, breathe deeply to relax as much as you can, then attempt to assess what is the truth of the matter at hand. This is hard because you typically get into the emotional realm which clouds your thinking. Then consider all of the resources you have at your disposal to address the problem. Include Spirit and your Higher Self... 200 feet, 150, 100...flare at 75, looking for 20 and 20 then 10 and 10…looks like we are going to make the field. Nailed it this time, wouldn't you say!" He sounded real pleased with himself.

"That's easy for you…"

"My auto?" He really was having fun with this.

Shaking my head, "No, relaxing and thinking through a crisis. It can be tough – I've found that training and preparation, so the solutions are right there, make it manageable."

"Well, it's not as hard as you may think."

"So, you're saying a crisis is just like an autorotation —you don't know when it will happen and when it does you follow the protocol and hope for the best…"

"Something like that."

"But that doesn't always work. Life is not that simple, neat and orderly, or even as logical and mechanical as an autorotation. Can't have a checklist or protocol for most things; it's ludicrous. After all, every situation is different."

"Agree. But also consider the possibility that a lot of what you experience in life are tests disguised as crisis. Crisis comes into your life when you need to have the experience—to learn from it. You attract the experience because your soul longs for it."

"Wait a minute - you mean to tell me that I create my own crises? I can sure think of a few I could have done without." I watched as Sam brought the helicopter around the field.

"Yes. I know, it's a tough one to swallow. There may be times when the soul wants to know if you've learned a lesson, so you're tested. If you have a series of similar crises, well, it may suggest that perhaps there is more learning to be done around the situation."

"I never thought that we attracted crisis into our lives."

"Hey, you are a helicopter pilot, right?"

"Right."

"Isn't facing the unexpected part of the reason you like flying? That's why you do autos all the time, when you can…right? Improves the odds, when you get a real one. Let's face it; you love passing tests! You love proving yourself. It's what pilots do!"

I had to consider this for a moment. Sam had a point, and not just airplane tests, but all tests. He was saying that life is one big test. He was right—I love a challenge. Who wouldn't?

"You remember talking about how the soul longs to be all that it can be, to discover itself, to create itself anew?"

"Yeah." That conversation still resonated in a big way.

"It's all about finding out what you can become in this life. Dealing with crisis is one of the fastest ways the soul can learn and grow. Think of it this way. The soul who comes into being on earth with a birth defect deals with crisis on a regular basis. The growth and mission of this soul is phenomenal, for it has chosen a lifetime of hardship—in other words, crisis to learn and grow from."

"So, I did not come in with anything like that. In fact, I'd say I've been really fortunate."

"But you came to experience life, to create and yes, you have had to deal with your share of crisis in your life, my friend, don't underestimate yourself. They have all been invaluable for your growth and development."

Sam continued, "Let's see…serious accident in 1958; trauma in 1962; placement in Spanish Elementary School in Peru without knowing the language; divorce in 1986; near death experience in 1990; car crash in 88; near drowning in Mexico in 1979, in-flight fire in 1978; and crash in 1981… leaving military service, heart operation, a couple of major career changes including becoming a healer…do I need to go on? And some you may not even know about… let's just say you "passed" these tests and many more, not to mention those in previous lifetimes." He stopped and glanced at me.

"Sam… how do you know this about me? You couldn't find all that, even on a Google search." I felt exposed somehow. Disadvantaged.

"Let's just say it's in the register."

"Register?"

"Okay, Robert, want to try a 180 auto?" We were approaching the south side of the field.

"Sure."

"You have the flight controls…"

"I have the controls."

Once abeam the field, I entered by lowering the collective and simultaneously rolling into a 180 degree right turn to line up on field. *Descent looks good. —1400 feet per minute… whoopee; speed a little fast… a little aft cyclic to get 60 knots… rapidly coming up on 75 feet, speed slowing—50… 40… 30… still descending ending coming up on 20 feet… 20 knots, level the nose a bit... 10 feet, pull collective 5…4... 3... 2... 1... touchdown.*

"Nice job! In the 180 as you bottom the collective on entry you have to add a little aft cycle as the nose wants to dip…you saw that with the speed increase, good catch. With the turn, the rate of descent will be slightly higher. Otherwise, the parameters remain the same as in a straight in. Ready for another?"

Sam and I continued to practice the autos till we had to return for fuel. It had been another interesting day.

Look at what is before your eyes. There are worthy and valuable blessings in every experience bringing new and unexpected good.

VIII

In the new energies, the now becomes the future.

We sat on the grass next to Gabriel eating sandwiches. Sam was very quiet as if he had something on his mind. I reflected on our talks and was surprised how comfortable I felt being with and talking with him. I'm pretty reserved and don't open up to many people right away. He had this uncanny ability to read me as if he knew the questions before I asked and the answer was precisely what I needed to hear. I had no clue where he was from and how he knew all these things about me—it was strange, but I trusted him, not knowing why.

"Sam, you talked about a register."

"Yes, the Akashic Records."

"Right, I have read about the Akashic Records and always wanted to know more."

"Good."

"So, as I understand it, these records are like a book."

"Correct. It's an energy, a vibration that's a record of all your past lifetimes, your growth, life goals, purpose. It even has goals that you may be planning for this lifetime. It is kept in a library, a place that exists in a higher dimension beyond this world. You can also access it within yourself through meditation."

Holy cow. I had to let this thought settle. The idea that every thought, belief, and everything past, present and future about my life and past lives was stored and available to me was hard to grasp. It was a tantalizing, scary thought.

"Do you mean to say that this information is always available to me. I can know everything about my past; and future?"

"Yes, let's just say you can reach and tap into this information; it's open."

"Just like that?"

"Correct. The Akashic Records are like a database of every word, thought or action that your soul has experienced, including the moment of its creation. It's an energetic blueprint of your soul's journey through its many lifetimes."

"So, how does it help me on my journey now?"

"Well, by accessing these records you can bring into your conscious awareness any latent gifts or strengths that you have, and also identify and release anything negative ones that you've created…"

I interrupted, "You mean karma, and any energetic blocks that are preventing me from moving forward on my journey?"

"Correct."

"So that also means any addictive patterns, relationship issues, and choices I've made will all be in the records?" I realized that this would be a patchwork of good and bad, some proud moments and some I'd like to forget.

"Precisely."

"How do I retrieve mine, Sam?"

"You have to ask yourself inside, and be specific about what you would like to know. I'll show you." He finished his sandwich and reached for his soda.

"First, you must set a clear intention on what you would like to know. Tuning into the records is a vibrational shift so that the vibration of your intention lines up and matches the vibration of the records."

My intent suddenly became clear in my mind.

"I would like to know about my soul's purpose in this lifetime."

"Good. Now take a few moments to close your eyes and center yourself in your heart, Robert. Feel unconditional love for yourself and the Masters, Teachers, and Loved Ones who will be working with you and the Akashic Records. The process of reading the records is you communing with the guides who are actively assigned to the region of the records being explored."

Flying With My Higher Self

I put my lunch down and settled myself leaning on Gabriel, closed my eyes and followed Sam's instructions. After a few minutes, "I feel like I am there."

"Not quite. Here let me help you."

Sam leaned over and placed his hand on my heart. I felt an energetic shift and a marvelous feeling of absolute love for myself as if I had a lotus flower that was blossoming in my heart center. It felt exquisite.

Sam sat back and continued, "It's really important to feel and be this love and gratitude as we access the records. Say after me: "I ask the Masters, Teachers and those who love me to share with me, Robert, and share whatever they wish about my records and that I will allow them to move this knowledge through me, out of higher realms, to say whatever they wish to help and guide me."

I repeated this out loud, phrase by phrase, a few times.

"Okay, now imagine a sphere of golden White Light around you. Make this Light beautiful, and see it surrounding your aura. Tell me when you have this."

"I'm there."

"Now imagine yourself rising higher and higher in this bubble, being carried into the higher dimensions. You are rising higher and higher now… higher and freer…higher and freer…"

"Yes, I feel freer and lighter now…"

"Good. Next, see yourself coming to the Great Library. You are standing in front of it. What does it look like?"

"I see a large stone building with a big wooden door –an entrance of sorts."

"Good. Enter that door and tell me what you see."

"I'm in a huge foyer or hall. There are many levels and each level has many doors."

"Do you see a door with your name on it?"

"No. I'll start at the first level and check."

"Take your time."

After a few minutes — taking long, deep breaths — Robert whispered, "I see it now."

"Describe it."

"It's gold with my name *Robert Rafael Maldonado* etched in black and silver cursive."

"Go ahead and open the door and tell me what you see."

"I see rows and rows of books and a podium with a large book on it. The book cover is brown and made of leather. It reads "The Book Of Life." These other books…are they also mine?"

"Yes, of your other lifetimes. Everyone's records are kept in this great library."

"When you're ready, open this book and look at the first page. What is written there?"

"It says: *A returning soul teaching humanity how to awaken to a higher consciousness with love, compassion.*"

"This is a dedication to the essence of your present life's work and the contribution you came to make in this lifetime. How does that feel to you?"

"Right. It rings true, the truth of who I am."

"Beautiful. Turn to the next page and tell me what it says."

I slowly read, the script seemed to float over the page, then summarized the words. "It says that I came to experience love towards myself, and to integrate my lifetimes and to serve others while exploring how this fits with the essence of who I am; something about being a way-shower and teacher. People will look to me and trust me."

"Right, more about your life's work and the contribution you came here to make. As you continue to access your Book of Life records, more will be revealed. You are doing great. Turn to the next page."

"I am seeing words…*integration, self-love, compassion, integrity, surrender, observe, joy, blissful unfoldment, trust, self-mastery…*"

"Very good…these are some of the qualities that you are working on developing more fully."

"Integration?"

"What does it say exactly, Robert?"

"Integration of different aspects of your soul from other lifetimes."

"This means that in this lifetime you are learning to harmonize and embrace all the experiences of other lifetimes. Perhaps, this is your purpose now. Let's go to the page that describes the most important events in your life thus far that have been recorded."

I carefully turned another few pages. "Born March 10, 1954 to Ralph Maldonado and Nydia Luisa Davila," I recited. All the episodes and occasions in my life were noted, in chronological order, including the present. It was fascinating to read. I flipped back a couple of pages and stumbled across a note, which I read aloud. "This Soul's first expression was in Arcturus, the star system." Wow, a different place altogether.

Sam didn't seem surprised. "You chose the Arcturus star system because you are most like the life forms there and are vibrationally aligned with the Arcturian energies. You could also say that your primary family on earth are Souls who are vibrationally in tune and harmonize with the Arcturus energies. In this lifetime, you have chosen to merge with your Galactic self—your star-seed and higher self. This is integration for you."

My mind was boggled. My brain seemed to have just stopped.

Sam went on, "Just so you know, the Akashic Records are the books that hold all of your past lives, ever since your Soul came into existence. *Your Book of Life* is the record of this present lifetime. The one you are living now. You can write into your Book of Life once you master this higher vibrational experience. Once this lifetime has ended, the current Book of Life is filed in with all of the other Akashic Records. But let's save this for another day. Okay, let's walk back through the door into the main library and through that door back to the bubble. Let me know when you are there." I complied automatically.

"Okay, I'm in the bubble."

"Allow the bubble to carry you back to where you are right now."

Afterwards, I felt as if I had been given a precious gift of remembrance and completion, discovering that I was fulfilling my Divine purpose and being of service. I still had many questions.

Resolve to be cheerful and helpful. People will repay you in kind.

IX

Answers to every question shall come
In some clear way,
Including quick and unexpected realizations,
Emerging from within.

"Okay, ready to practice running landings?"

We had already been flying for a while doing takeoff and landings and Sam's favorite, auto-rotations, he said "just to warm up."

"Running landings are pretty simple in the 47. We do them simulating a maximum gross weight and high density-altitude environment. It's a good option when power is critical and you have a nice field or runway to land on. I'll shoot a normal approach and instead of coming to a complete stop I'll just slide in at 5-10 knots groundspeed. Of course, you already know this."

There he goes again.

"Okay, we're at 300 feet and 50 knots on base leg to final approach …I am turning to final for my approach, got my sight picture… looking good … now… lowering the collective to begin a descent keeping 3100 rpm and looking for 50 knots. There we go…50 knots. I'll set 300-400 feet per minute rate of descent on the vertical velocity indicator (VVI) and keep the 50 knots till approximately 50 feet when I'll add a little back cyclic to bleed off speed. At 10 feet, I adjust the nose slightly to the landing attitude and hold this looking for 5-10 knots groundspeed to touchdown. You may have to improvise based on conditions."

After coming to a full stop Sam asked, "Questions?"

"No."

"Okay, you have the controls. Let's give her a whirl. I'll talk you through it."

"I have the controls."

I flew a standard traffic pattern and began practicing running landings. Sam and I alternated. One of them felt different and I wasn't sure why till after I came to a full stop.

"Well, Cowboy…you really broke the *record* on that last one." Sam said looking at me almost beaming incredulously.

"What do you mean?"

"Your touch down speed…I thought you were plowing the field for farmer Joe there."

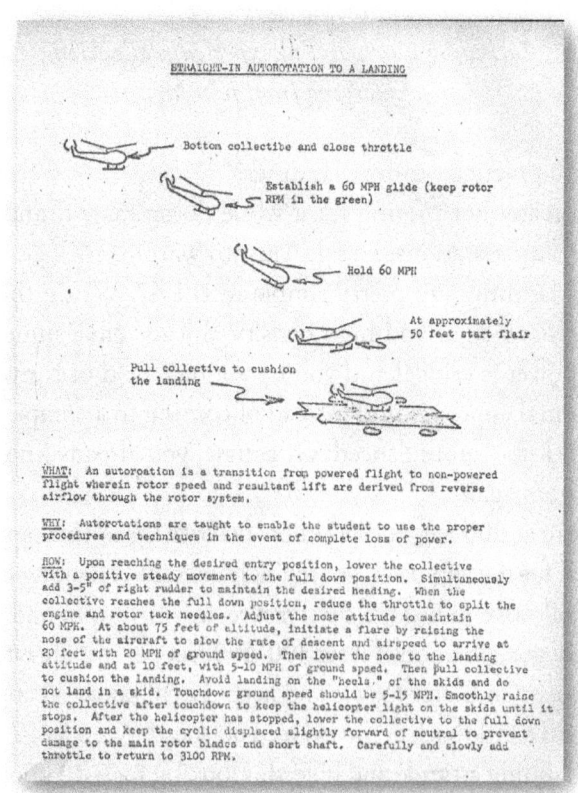

Running Landing

Flying With My Higher Self

"What!"

"It was over 40 knots, 43 to be exact!"

"Whoa, I'm really sorry. Guess I wasn't paying attention…didn't realize…"

"You looked pretty intent on keeping the speed, that's why I left you alone. Otherwise it was the *smoothest* and *fastest* landing I have seen in the 47! Seriously, maybe one for the record books. Glad the surface was smooth. A rougher field and it would have been real sporty!"

"I must have been somewhere else Sam… why didn't you stop me…take the controls?" I said, frustrated and surprised.

"Didn't have to. You created the experience, Robert, or let's say *re-created* it."

All of a sudden, I felt a flash of light, really bright …blinding… and felt myself slowly drifting back in time…

February 1978; over the South China Sea in the cockpit of a U.S. Marine Corps Sikorsky CH-53D Sea Stallion helicopter with 30 combat loaded Marines and internal fuel tank strapped under the main gearbox. We were headed to South Korea from Okinawa as part of the annual Team Spirit exercise supporting the Republic of Korea (ROK) Marines.

Suddenly, flying at 500 feet and 110 knots, there was a loud noise followed by a series of bangs and a shudder that rocked the giant helicopter. At first, I thought…bird strike—we hit something.

Me: "What was that?"

Co-pilot: "Captain, the #1 engine is spoiling down, temp rising fast."

Me: "Roger…confirm engine."

Crew Chief: "Roger, sir, it's # 1 …throttles coming full forward."

AVIATE, NAVIGATE, COMMUNICATE!

Me: "Coming back to single engine airspeed of 80 knots."

Crew Chief: "Temps rising…got smoke in the cabin. Will go back to check it out!"

Copilot: "Descending sir."

Me: "Check for fire."

A few minutes later, Crew Chief: "We're okay, nothing back here. Must have been the exhaust released from the engine, # 1 temp rising still. Guys back here are a little nervous."

Me: Run emergency checklist for engine failure: (This is a challenge and response by other crewmembers.)

Crew Chief doing the run-down:

"Throttles: FULL FORWARD."

"Check copilot."

"Airspeed –80 Knots."

"Check pilot."

"Throttle SHUTOFF on #."

"Check co-pilot." (Confirms # 1 to avoid shutting down good engine). Crew chief moves selector lever.

"Fuel Selector Switch—OFF."

"Check co-pilot."

"Ignition Switch—OFF."

"Check co-pilot."

"Fire extinguisher—MAIN/RESERVE."

Me: "Not required."

Crew Chief: "Attempt Restart Sir?"

Me: "Negative."

Copilot: "Amami Island is 15 miles away right about 45 degrees. Map shows it has a commercial runway."

Me: "Roger, let's get their tower frequency, coming right. VHF 123.5."

Crew Chief: "123.5 in radio."

Me: "Amami Tower, Lion 14."

(Japanese controller in accented English) "Lion 14…, this is Amani Tower, good morning."

"Roger, Lion 14, Marine Corps CH-53 heavy helicopter declaring emergency engine failure, 15 miles SW at 400 feet. Would like the runway, if available."

Copilot: "300 feet sir."

Me: "Roger, I will keep 80 knots for now."

Crew Chief: "#1 engine shutdown checklist completed."

Me: "Okay, keep an eye on the temps and rpm." *Shit…# 2 engine…. what's that?... flickering caution light on panel…hang in there.*

Flying With My Higher Self

Crew Chief: "Doing power computation…"
Amami Tower responds,
"Lion 14…runway 18 is active, are you declaring emergency?"
Me: "Lion 14…affirmative."
Tower: "Lion 14, you are cleared to land…winds 160/5 knots. Report field in sight. Air Nippon 34 hold position, emergency in progress…Air New Zealand 76 contact ground 145.7. Good day."
Me: "Okay will attempt running landing. Landing checklist."
Keep speed up a bit in case you lose #2. Damn…# 2 engine fuel caution light flickering again.
Me: "Let team leader in back know that we're diverting due to emergency."
Co-pilot: "Sir, I have the runway in sight, come right 20 degrees."
Me: "Coming right."
Crew Chief: "Landing Checklist: "THROTTLES—FULL FORWARD. GEAR-DOWN."
The sound of landing gear coming down, strangely reassuring.
Crew Chief: "Three down and locked, landing checklist complete. Power available: 101; required 90."
A little margin, not much.
Co-pilot: "Gear checked down."
Approaching the field and minutes later, then, "Runway in sight, on final approach."
Me: "Amami Tower, Lion 14 has field in sight."
Tower: "Roger, Lion 14, you are cleared to land. Emergency equipment standing by."
I knew the CH-53 emergency procedure for a single engine running landing: starts at 80 knots with a gradual deceleration, making sure touch down is no faster than 40 knots to avoid blowing the tires. Landing attitude is 10 degrees max to avoid the tail striking the ground.
Me: "I'm going to keep speed up all the way down guys."
Crew chief: "Looks like we have #2 fuel light on caution panel. Reset."
Me: "Roger…keep an eye on it…on final approach."
Copilot: "70 knots…60…50…"

Over runway threshold, "Slightly above 40 knots …" The TAIL SKID WARNING HORN caution light and warning horn comes on (warning to not exceed 10 degree nose attitude or we will hit tail).

Keep speed up just in case you lose #2 and have to do an autorotation.

Crew chief pushes reset on caution panel to turn light off "below 40 …10 feet…5 feet…touchdown."

I hear the sounds of landing as the Crew Chief says, "Nice one sir."

Me, releasing the breath I didn't know I was holding, "After Landing Checklist, please."

We continued down the runway and taxied into the ramp and shutdown followed by the airport fire and rescue trucks.

Crew chief: "After landing complete sir."

Me, "Thank you."

I was beginning to feel my body again. Sam watched me; he understood.

"Okay, hotshot, you had one of those moments. We all get them, you know."

"So, somehow Gabriel One Zero was Lion 14…How can that be and why the experience again?"

"At some level you re-created the experience, an affirmation perhaps of skills you have mastered. Maybe even a test. Remember, it's because you fly helicopters Robert."

"Right, but I did not pass the test if I came in that fast!"

"Well, we survived. Let's just say there was a reason for it. Just accept it. You were in a parallel dimension Robert, in a special NOW moment where there is no past or future or linear time. Do you remember the # 2 engine?"

"What about it?"

"The maintenance crew replaced the one that failed and flew the helicopter back to your base. Enroute, the #2 fuel light came on and *that* engine failed. It was shut down and the pilots flew on the remaining engine (the new one they'd just put in) to a full stop landing. You were lucky. Had that #2 failed on you earlier, it may have been a completely different outcome. It was good thinking to ask for the runway and to have kept your speed up. They found contaminated fuel in the tanks."

"Yeah, I remember it was acting strangely…the flickering fuel flow gauge and light on the caution panel."

"What else do you remember Robert?"

"Well, later after we taxied in to park there was a lot of confusion. The airport manager who spoke no English was not happy to see us. Apparently, we had landed at a Japanese resort island and he resented having 30 U.S. Marines in full combat gear on his ramp. Not good for tourism. Can't say that I blamed him. I remember that we were visited by a Japanese airline captain, short, stocky guy with white hair—looked to be in mid 60s, who spoke perfect English. He was very interested in the helicopter so we showed him around."

"What else do you remember about him?"

"Well, he had the most gentle and polite manner, a real gentlemen, and he smiled a lot. He stepped in to help mediate with the airport manager who was really pissed off. After that things got better."

"Yes, he was all of that and more. Mr. Iroshi Yamato, Air Nippon senior Captain, age 63, Buddhist monk and Japanese ace of World War II fame; married 3 kids—2 lawyers and a doctor. Comes from a long lineage of Samurai warriors and Shinto priests. Impressive guy. During the war he flew from the same airfield you landed on. How's that for coincidence. You have a lot in common. But it gets better."

Sam continued, "Towards the end of the war, when the Japanese naval pilot shortage was acute, he volunteered to become a Kamikaze suicide pilot to fly out to the American fleet and crash into the ships during the Okinawa campaign. It was to be his last contribution to the war, a final mission to bestow honor to Japan and his family. He was already somewhat of a legend at the time. His superiors reluctantly consented. However, something happened to Iroshi on that last mission, because he brought his badly shot up plane back to Amami, landing on what is runway 18 now. That feat in itself was a miracle. Very few if any suicide pilots returned. Iroshi, for all practical purposes, was a changed man after that. He died in 1993 and kept the secret of what happened to him on that day to his death."

"As you came in to land, Captain Yamato in Air Nippon 34, holding at end of runway in a Boeing 737-300, heard your distress call with the tower and was praying for you. He put a column of golden-white light around you and your aircraft to ensure you landed safely."

"All I remember was that the landing was effortless as if I had some unseen force helping me…So, he also knew about the # 2 engine."

"Yes."

"I am very grateful. How can I thank Captain Yamato for what he did that day?"

Pause.

"You'd honor him by learning to do what he did."

"What?"

"It's easier than you think. First, let's talk about light. There is a part of you that comes from the Stars. Yes, you are a star traveler—a star seed, Robert. Science today is finding that you are made of stardust—silica to be exact. How's that for a concept. A crystalline body of light, an upgraded version of your carbon-based one! Ever have days when you have looked up at the stars and felt 'Home,' because that's where you came from my friend."

"Yes, sometimes."

"Well, you are light. It's a potent force of transformation and transmutation. With the new energies coming in now, you can strengthen your connection to your higher self. You can call on this light to transmute energy and to empower and heal yourself and others. Captain Yamato knew this."

"How does this happen?"

"First, you must believe that you are Light. Then, call it upon yourself to link into its energy, harness its power. Light increases your vibration, amplifies your energy and the strength of your positive thoughts. It opens your heart and creates good all around you."

"Just like that?"

"Right, stop for a moment and call light to yourself."

"How?"

"I have the controls. I am going to show you something. I want you to see yourself connecting with the light. Invite it to come to you Robert. This light is living consciousness that responds instantly to your call. Imagine a column of light entering your spine and going to your feet, going into your cells, DNA and throughout your body. Just feel this now. Completely fill your body with this beautiful light."

After a moment, there is a pause as I feel the Light in me.

"How does that feel?"

A few minutes go by.

"I feel lighter, freer, expansive…warm, peaceful and a feeling of love."

"Good, you are connecting with the Light energy. Now, I want you to imagine this light as a sphere or cone all around you, in front and back, above the head and below the feet. Make this sphere radiate out—making it larger so it includes Gabriel; and, if you can outside as far as you want. What does that feel like?"

"Sam, I feel energized, charged, expansive and a peace within that's hard to describe."

"Good. Now think of sending it out. It could be you send it to a friend, loved one, your future, your higher purpose in this lifetime, your thoughts, pains, whatever. By doing this you transform and change the energy of whatever you send it to into a higher vibration. I call it co-creating with light like an artist using paint on a canvas."

"I have a friend who is very sick now…"

"Okay, so you first become the light by infusing yourself with it, which you have. Now you have called the light to yourself and charged yourself with it. You embody the light becoming a pure transmitter of light. Next, you send light to this person through your whole body by imagining it coming out of your eyes, hands or heart and going directly to that person. See that person in the golden white Light."

I take a few minutes to feel this.

"How does that feel?"

"I feel it going to her."

Sam adds, "Good, I can see her surrounded by this bluish-white light."

"So, you have learned how to call the light to yourself, charge yourself with it and radiate it out. Practice this as much as you can. Connect with the light during the day, at work, in the car, at home, in the store. As you connect with the light you become a bridge between yourself and the higher realms and become more radiant and heart-centered."

"Do you think this will improve my performance flying, at some future event?"

"Give it a shot."

I am smiling now. "Okay, I am going to send Light to myself and the field where I am going to do my next running landing."

"Okay, whenever you are ready. What is your intention going to be?"

"To make it the best one I have done all morning."

"Open your eyes. You have the controls."

"I have the controls."

And sure enough, my landing was not only effortless but it *was* the best one I had ever done. Period. Sam was pleased.

"Okay, let's go around and do a few more running landings and remember 5-10 knots …Okay?"

"Right!"

You are the Light from the Heavens; Call Light to yourself and share your Light with others!

X

No one gets out of this world alive.
Resolve then to maintain
A reasonable sense of values.

Once again, Sam and I were back in the airport café. The friendly waitress approached us as two old friends.

"Good to see you gents again. Do you need menus or do you already know what you want?"

"Turkey Club for me, on wheat toast, and whatever my partner wants, it's on my check."

"Yes sir."

"I would like the same please, but no cheese. Also, a sweet tea for me."

"You sir."

"Just water."

"Okay, thanks."

"Sam, you had mentioned that the light increases your vibration. As a pilot, I've learned to tune into vibration and approach it with caution."

Sam leaned forward, elbows on the table. "You got that right. Everything in our Universe vibrates. Everything is energy in motion with a resonant frequency ranging from the most dense to the least dense. Call it God's essence."

"I understand that everything is energy and that we are vibratory beings of light made in the image of the creator."

Sam added, "...and as you know we're surrounded by a field of energy, an aura, that pulsates at the frequency of the light quotient within us."

"You lost me on the last one. What do you mean by light quotient?"

"It's a measure of the lights vibration, the light energy that you carry in you. The higher the quotient the more your life resonates with purpose, focus, harmony."

"So, we need to keep our vibrational rate high." I watched a young family move to a table near the window. "How?"

"Let me give you an analogy. You've heard the saying that helicopter pilots literally beat the air into submission to fly as we vibrate (laughing)." I smiled at that old analogy. "We're instinctively attuned to vibrations and know when things are not in balance. Agree?"

Me and my crew chief know about that firsthand, I thought.

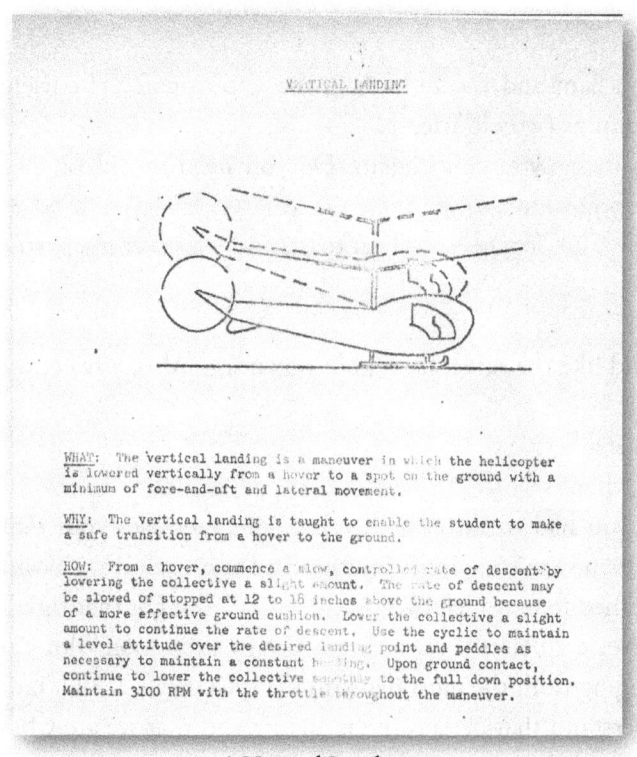

A Vertical Landing

"Yes."

Sam continued, "So, Gabriel here is a complex assembly of highly vibrating components that are in balance (hopefully) and that give it unique flight characteristics that are unavailable to fixed wing airplanes. Helicopters are sensitive to imbalances so we're always making sure that they vibrate in their design frequency, for the safety and longevity of the helicopter and crew."

The waitress set two plates, our drinks and an assortment of condiments down. "Dessert is apple dumplings or lemon cake. Enjoy!" We watched her head to the family, menus in hand.

Sam reached for his water. "The same applies to us. The human body also has a resonant frequency that is optimum for health and wellbeing. And as you increase your consciousness, we increase our capacity to assimilate and bring in more light. The cliché is that we're light beings having an earth experience. We bring in light to ourselves to experience our light in the third dimension."

As an energy healer, this sounded familiar but I felt the opportunity to ask what I had sometimes wondered about, "How do I know what my resonant frequency is?"

"Great question."

"You'll know it when you open your heart. You raise your vibration by opening your heart to the love of God within you. When you feel this love, you can't help but experience more aliveness, expansion, renewal, oneness. Love is the resonant vibration of the universe. As above, so below. It's who we are. As you learn to love yourself and become this love, your vibration increases. Your energy also takes on the smoother, higher vibrations of the higher dimensions and you become your Higher Self.

I held up my hand. "Wait a minute. That's a lot to digest."

Sam said, "It's not complicated. Because everything in the universe has a vibration, the rate of your vibration determines the people, events, circumstances, that you attract to yourself."

"So, loving myself not only raises my vibration but also allows me to love others."

"Precisely, and as you love others you raise your vibration and attract good things into your life as well. It is truly a gift that you give to yourself as you give to others."

I hesitated momentarily reflecting on what he had said. 'Love your neighbor as thy self. Now I understood it.'

"Sam, I've had a difficult time loving myself in this lifetime."

"Yeah, I know. You're too hard on yourself -- set high standards and expect the same of others, yet this has shrouded you with doubt, fear, anger and in some ways closed your heart to life."

"I know. It's been one of my hardest lessons."

"It comes from expecting perfection in life, which is impossible. You strive for it and its expected in your culture. That's the illusion."

"You mean perfection."

"Striving to be perfect, and not remembering that you already are. Big difference."

"I never felt enough…"

"That's right, and you compensated beautifully by creating an idealized self-image of who you wanted the world to see; Robert as—successful, competent, strong, and not weak, vulnerable, or unreliable. That came at the expense of your authenticity and true essence. You get my drift?"

"Right. I wasted more energy resisting and not recognizing who I truly am."

"You are not alone here. The biggest problem humanity faces is that they do not remember who they really are. They resist and believe they are something *less* than what they really are. It's not that you are not awake, but that you forget that you already are."

"Yeah, that's right. But that's also the amazing thing. Now that I've retired and let go of that so-called striving for success, I've opened up to more of myself. I feel as if I have awakened and remembered who I AM."

"That's great. Cause once you can let go and begin to love your imperfections, and insecurities, you can accept them as a part of who you are. Remember, you came here to explore a frequency. You don't change that by denying or hating parts of yourself. In fact, people can spend a lot of time and energy pretending, resisting and defending."

"I know, it can be wearisome – always being "on" or something."

Sam continued, "It's about loving your humanity as well as your divinity. Remember you are a divine being having an earth experience. Love all your experiences, and I mean ALL of them without judgment. You are already perfect, Robert!"

I laughed. "It's a different lesson than we get in school or in church loving everything about ourselves, the good and bad."

"I wouldn't call it good or bad. Love everything about you. Love your weaknesses as well as your strengths, talents and gifts without any judgment."

"Accepting my weaknesses has always been a challenge for me."

"Consider your weaknesses as the areas that you need to evolve and as you love them you will find that your world expands and your choices increase. Makes sense?"

"Yes. I've been working on this, accepting my whole self and opening my heart center to bring more love in to my life and to balance my energies. I'm getting better at it."

"Good. Okay, let's try something. Put your hand over your heart and say to yourself, *I, Robert, love me and accept me as I AM.* Now, feel the truth and energy of this in your heart."

"I, Robert, love me and accept me as I AM."

"Repeat after me. I ask my heart to guide me in a loving way and to give me the strength to listen to it clearly and to trust it."

"I ask my heart to guide me in a loving way and to give me the strength to listen to it clearly and to trust it."

"Good. Imagine your heart as a star and let it radiate love and light to every cell of your body. Feel this light balancing, harmonizing and regenerating throughout your body now. Feel its life force awakening all the cells in your body.

"Now, spend a moment feeling the emotions that are coming up for you right now. Send love to each one you identify. Do the same for any thoughts that come up now. Send love to each thought."

"Take a deep breath."

Afterwards, I felt a blissful peace that I had not felt in a long time.

XI

*There will be changes and detours to the
flight plan—that's part of the game.*

The next day, after flying, we drove into town for dinner. Ben's Diner was reputed to have the best burgers and sandwiches in the area. A change from the airport café sounded good. And, as was typical, we talked about flying, different helicopters, pilots we'd known, war stories and burgers. Then, I turned to what had been on my mind for a while.

"Sam, how have you found your way forward in your spiritual growth? I'm kind of floundering and question sometimes if I'm not bogged down somehow."

"Well, let me think – nourishing the soul is different for everyone. There's no one answer."

"No, you're right; it's not one size fits all." I added.

Sam chimed in, "When I've found myself in an empty space – and sometimes it takes a while to realize it – I ask a question like: Has my soul learned all of its lessons in this lifetime and if not, what is blocking the way forward. Sometimes just finding the right question can open a new window for you."

"I've done the same thing, with just about the same questions. And I haven't gained any new insights. I feel pretty good about my life now; things are going well for me. I am at peace with myself and am unaware of any blocks or new defenses. However, it just feels like I'm coasting."

"Maybe, just maybe, you're where you are meant to be. Maybe, you're fulfilling your purpose, and the peace and harmony you are experiencing now is a reflection of that."

"Maybe. Feels incomplete, though."

"Your soul is always evolving, Robert, and that happy spot of peace is part of that, part of experiencing the light within. As you know, the duality of this dimension is a very difficult place to be, but a great place to learn soul lessons."

"Yeah. I've had my share, Sam. Military, teacher, healer, writer, husband, partner, son, friend, brother and lots of experiences in each. They felt like challenges and tests."

"Your soul has already learned invaluable lessons then. It also knows what lessons it's here to accomplish and the experiences it needs to have."

"Sounds like predestination."

"No predestination suggests a predetermined outcome. Look at it another way. Maybe the soul evaluates potential paths to explore, paths that would present the lessons it needed to learn. As we have discussed, one of the lessons of your soul is to integrate various lifetimes, to express its soul's energy and share its presence. And that's through your awareness of your higher self."

"I am glad you brought the higher self into this. Asking for guidance from my higher self is a big part of my meditation. Some days I get something in the quiet space, but not always. Usually through some un-expected phrase or intuition. Or through some odd coincidence or synchronicity; people, books, movies that send a message that suddenly I'm ready to get. I've found my higher self is like a growing life-force consciousness that is part of me but is fully aware of me, the soul, and the God that is within me. I can't explain it well."

Sam gazed off into space, "Wonderful awareness, Robert. The higher self is the core or essence of who you are and holds the accumulated knowledge from all your lifetimes, because it's been with you in each of these lifetimes. It is like a very wise teacher *within* you. It knows love, harmony, order and light and reminds you that this is the essence of who you are, Robert. It is your expanded, loving wise, and compassionate self."

Flying With My Higher Self

Sam paused momentarily while biting into his sandwich.

"Your goal is to communicate with your higher self and to move your higher self presence into your physical body. Then you will be a walking ascended being. More on that later."

How do I know that it is communicating with me and not another voice?"

"The higher self usually talks to you through your intuition and feelings. It also communicates with you like you said through events like coincidences and synchronicity —in the forms of people, books, movies, newspapers and things that give you messages that it wants you to know. The higher self knows all the challenges you face in your life and sends you impulses to be loving and united with others."

"So, when I have been in my heart—heart-centered and doing things with love and focus, getting creative insights, working with the light, serving and making a difference in the lives of others, I have been communicating with my higher self?"

"That's right. You ask yourself: 'How can I contribute to the higher good of myself and others?' That is being in your higher self. And the higher self communicates through a gentle, loving sense of knowing."

"I know. It always feels better. Sometimes, I can feel when I'm acting from lower self, the little hard ego. Everyone needs it to some degree – the ego keeps you safe and teaches you the ways of the world. But it also keeps track of all past hurts and wounds and holds on to fear and guilt. And judgment."

"Well said."

"So, what kind of signal would I get from my lower self?"

"Like you said, the messages you get from your lower self are often fearful and based on thoughts of scarcity, guilt, or a need to protect yourself from some imagined threat."

"So what form does a signal from my higher self look like?"

"It depends on how you sense energy. You are kinesthetic, so will experience a feeling or some sense of knowing. Some people get colors or have visual experiences, others hear it. Allow your connection to broaden and practice.

How about we try this. Close your eyes and ask your higher self to communicate a 'yes' to you."

I slowly closed my eyes.

"I can feel a pleasurable opening in my heart."

"Good. Now ask your higher self to give you a signal for No."

"I felt a closing or contraction energy in my heart."

"There you go. So, when you ask your higher self a question, your answers will come through a heart feeling. This is one way. Generally, the higher self will communicate in a gentle, inviting, open, loving and positive way. Be open. In some cases, it may be a knowing or thought."

I stopped for a moment. All this conversation left me with the warm glow I felt in meditation when I was close to my higher self. "But Sam, it's often difficult to distinguish the voice of the intellect or ego and the higher self."

"True. The voice of the higher self is often subtle and quiet and is frequently the first message you hear. The intellect will jump in with answers, perhaps on a certain action that you must take, but that may not be coming from your higher self. For messages from your higher self, get silent and go within and wait until you sense the answer that is reassuring and loving. Remember, the quiet voice of the higher self is always encouraging and positive."

He paused and then continued, "It's all about growing through connecting with your higher self. And aligning with and becoming that higher self—to feel your higher self as *you*."

"I see. But how?"

"Okay. Close your eyes. Get comfortable. Now, take three deep breaths to clear your mind and to ground your energies."

I began to relax.

"I want you to imagine a stream of golden-white light energy coming up through the soles of your feet, then up the calves and thighs, rising slowly… then up your abdomen, lower back and then the upper back, shoulders, going from your shoulders to your elbows forearms, and hands, then back up to your neck, head and face. Allow all the muscles and organs in your body to feel this wonderful, warm energy flowing through it. Do this until you feel peaceful, focused and comfortable."

A few minutes later I murmured, "I am there."

"Good, now imagine that you are in the center of a large circle and you are surrounded by the most translucent beings of light who are standing in a circle around you. Feel their peace, love and joy. They are going to assist you in meeting your higher self."

"It feels wonderful."

"Imagine the higher self in the distance, beginning to come towards you. Tell me what you see."

"I can see a being…with a shimmering white light moving towards me."

"When you meditate, and are feeling the peace and love of Spirit, invite your higher self to come closer. Feel its radiance, its living energy beginning to surround you and embrace you now. Ask your higher self to assist you in making a stronger connection."

"I can feel these cords or lines of light coming from my higher self and my vibration increasing—like I am expanding and I am becoming one with— merging with it."

"Wonderful, stay with this feeling."

Later, that evening, in my meditation I focused on loving my higher self. I didn't really ask anything except to feel its presence. Just as Sam had said, it was there. I felt as though I was reacquainting myself with a part of me, an old and dear friend. And out of the blue, the strange coincidence of finding Sam when I did struck me. It was one of those unexpectedly rich friendships that pushed me forward.

I almost said it out loud, "Sam…I am seeing myself…different aspects… of lives being revealed to me. I can see my past lives and there is a life with you. Somewhere, you and I were, or have been, together before."

Then clearly, quietly, I heard, "We have, Robert."

Robert R. Maldonado, PhD

QUICK STOPS (RAPID DECELERATIONS)

- 50 feet, 50-60 MPH
- decrease collective, slight back pressure on cyclic
- continue down collective & back cyclic to decrease groundspeed
- forward cyclic & up collective
- settle to a normal hover

QUICK STOP

WHAT: The quick stop is a rapid deceleration of the helicopter; altitude, heading, and RPM remain constant throughout the attitude change.

WHY: The quick stop is taught to develop coordination and to enable the student to stop the helicopter rapidly while in forward flight.

HOW: From a five-foot hover, commence a normal transition to forward flight. When reaching 40-60 feet and 40-60 MPH of forward airspeed, reduce airspeed, reduce the collective to 20" MAP, and assume a level attitude. Coordinate down collective with aft cyclic to slow the helicopter while maintaining a constant altitude. Maintain 3100 RPM with proper throttle pressure and maintain a constant heading with peddle. Recover in a hover attitude.

Quick Stop Procedure

XII

*You look at where you are in life— Bringing
in different kinds of backgrounds.
You are on an invisible, uncharted path,
which you will discover day by day.*

Another sunny, gorgeous day. We'd done the preflight and were settling into the cockpit, helmets in hand. "Ready for your check-ride?"

"What check-ride?"

"That's right."

"You're joking. I…we've only flown, maybe, 6 hours or so…"

"You're ready Robert."

"Well…okay, let's go."

He sat back and looked at me, deliberately. "I've been thinking, I'd like you to take over for me…flying Gabriel here, and I just need to make sure you are ready and safe."

"Sam, I am not sure that's in my plan right now. Besides…"

Sam interrupted. "I understand. Just think about it, Okay, I'm getting a little old for this, you know, hand and foot coordination, eyesight, hearing… and all that other stuff that comes with aging. You get my drift."

For a moment, I wondered if I had missed a sign of something seriously wrong. "Is everything all right?"

"Oh, yeah, of course. Ready to go?"

"As ready as I can be."

"Okay, Robert, let's run through the start-up sequence together. Ask anything, just pretend I'm your copilot. You run the checklist and I'll assist. Ready?"

I nodded affirmative and started down the engine start checklist.

"Take off checklist." We ran through the items.

"Checklist complete."

"Very good. Okay, I have the controls."

Sam lifted Gabriel to 5 feet and we hover-taxied to the edge of the airfield adjacent the runway. "Show me a constant heading square, Robert."

"Roger, I have the controls."

I hovered the helicopter with the forward tips of the landing gear over the corner of a white lined square in the grass.

"Very good, now do a parallel heading square."

I hovered the helicopter with the forward tips of the landing skids over the corner of the square, then moved the helicopter forward executing a 90 degree turn at each corner until we were back to the starting position.

"Very nice. Let's do a normal takeoff and transition into the pattern."

"Tower, good morning Rita…Gabriel One Zero request takeoff, will stay in the pattern."

"Gabriel One Zero, good morning to you Sam…and Robert, right? Roger, cleared for takeoff… winds 180/5 knots. You requested pattern?"

"Roger Tower."

"Roger, One Zero, cleared for the pattern."

I lifted Gabriel and increased power while keeping 3100 rpm and beginning a gradual climb to 500 feet at 50 knots.

As we leveled off Sam said, "Hey Robert, I have the controls. I am not sure I demoed the parameters for a local traffic pattern. Pretty straight forward as you will see. By the way…nice takeoff."

"You have the controls."

Sam executed a level turn to our downwind leg staying at 500 feet and 60 knots. On the base leg, he began a descent to 300 feet and 50 knots. "I just hold 300/50 on the base leg. I then do a level turn to final approach keeping these parameters till I have my sight picture, then begin my descent for the helipad —about 12-degree glide slope with constant deceleration to a hover. You have a go. You have the controls."

"I have the controls."

I went around the pattern a few times doing takeoffs and landings. On the fourth or fifth pass, I returned to an earlier conversation. "Sam, the other day you said that one of the lessons of the soul is to integrate various lifetimes, to express its soul's energy and share its presence."

"Yeah."

"What did you mean by integration and bringing in past lifetimes?"

He paused before answering. "From the soul's perspective, you've had many lifetimes. I'd venture to say that you know some of these already…right?"

"Why yeah, I think so.…I know that I was a high priest in Atlantis, an architect and priest in Egypt, a monk in Italy during the Renaissance era, a warrior in the Lydra constellation and many others. I believe I've been a warrior, teacher and healer in many other lifetimes. Guess it's my pattern."

"Yes, and small correction—you've had thousands of lifetimes on this earth and other planets. I can attest to that." He chuckled. "Your soul has manifested in many Earth lifetimes because the soul wanted to experience all aspects that are possible in the self in the third dimension. You are an "old" soul, literally."

I made a turn to base leg for the approach.

Sam continued, "And your soul-higher self is like a pie. Each slice of the pie contains a different part of your higher self-soul from a different lifetime."

"So, the goal then is to unify all of these experiences and to get synergy, not just a compilation."

"Exactly, you've got it. You said that you had been a warrior, teacher and healer in previous lifetimes."

"Yeah, I think so."

"Since you have been all of these, maybe even a woman in other lifetimes, consider the possibility that you could choose to unify any and all these lifetimes in one lifetime. That is what we mean by integration. Hold the thought for a moment Robert. Let's do a few auto-rotations."

"I have the controls."

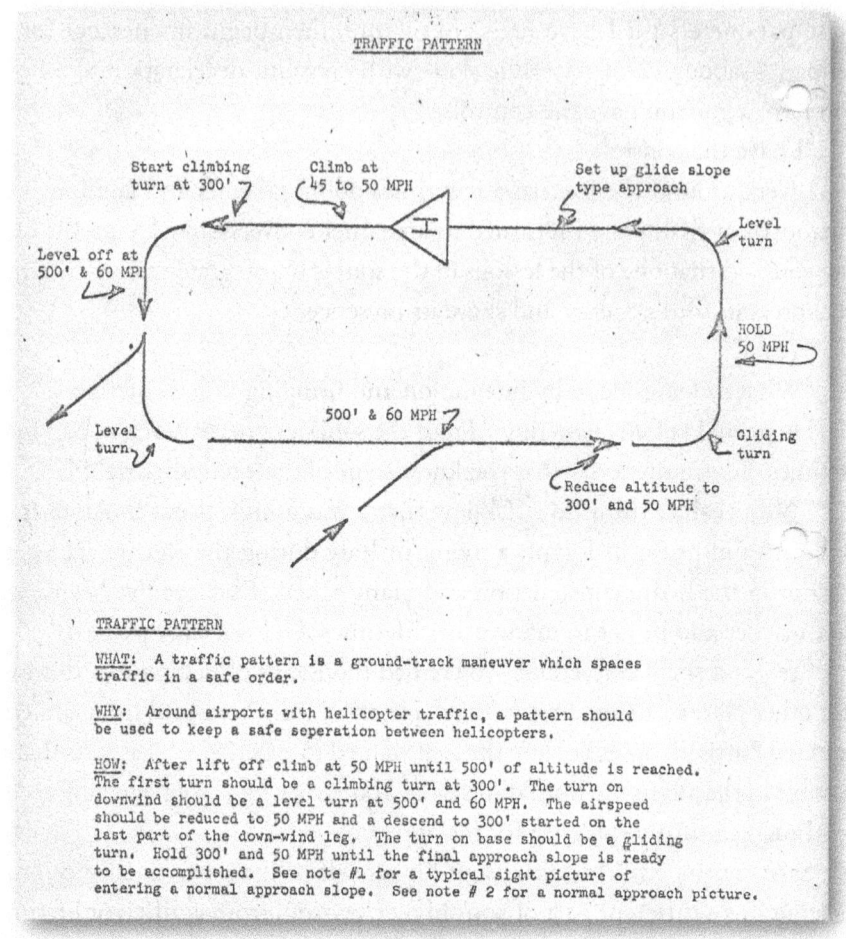

Traffic Pattern

We climbed to 1000 feet over the airfield and Sam entered into a 180 degree autorotation while executing a controlled landing. We alternated back and forth. Sam was very quiet. Unusually quiet.

"Hey Sam, what if you're not aware of your past lives. How does integration work there?"

"Good question. I use knowledge of the past as an example of integration, to make a point. But you don't have to look at past lives to do this."

"You lost me."

"Just look at what is going on in this lifetime. Focusing on the Now moment. You could ask yourself, 'What issues or situations are playing out in my life now? What patterns am I reacting to that are not serving my highest good?'"

"Makes sense."

"Sure, the past life can be useful and give you another perspective. It could tell you that you tried something a certain way and that's how it worked out, and that perhaps you find yourself repeating this same pattern. But you don't need that knowledge for integration."

"So, the higher self is saying 'never mind' and let's focus on the Now moment."

"I couldn't have said it any better!"

"In fact, as I understand it, a past life is really not past."

"That's right. In the higher dimensions, time doesn't exist. Past, present, future is all going on concurrently. Time, is a third dimensional construct to enable experience and learning."

"So, what I am doing in the Now, let's say integrating a past life in this lifetime, is affecting that past lifetime."

"Brilliant. I can see you are going to do great when you take over for me. What you experienced in the 'past' lifetime, say guilt or shame or other wound, comes forward (or sideways) into this lifetime and may manifest in different ways. Since the past and present are concurrent then you can apply lessons from that lifetime allowing for deeper healing and integration."

"So, I have healed my past as well."

"Your past and also your entire genetic line. They can choose to download it for learning purposes as well or choose not to."

"I like the concept of healing all generations including future ones. I know that I grew up with lots of self-esteem issues, as the oldest in my family not feeling good enough, closing my feelings, some fear and regret. I feel as if I have healed much of this in this lifetime and learned the lessons and integrated these."

"Yes, you have. Additionally, by doing so you have also healed your family and generational line. So, let's look at this lifetime. Consider the possibility that you came back in this lifetime to be here in this precise moment of the earth's evolution to unify your higher self-soul. As you said, you have been a warrior, teacher and healer in many lifetimes and have also been all of those in this lifetime. Does this suggest anything to you?"

"Well, sure, that this is a real gift and wonderful opportunity for me now."

"Yes. The whole point of your experiences is integration. The soul is evolving on a path of remembering through learning. As you go through the process of ascension, you are bringing 'home' all aspects of yourself that you still perceive as separate. Forgiving yourself for the things that you've done in other lifetimes while acknowledging the wonderful things that you've done—this is the integration process. Your goal is to communicate with your higher self and to move your higher self –essence, your purified true self, into your physical body. Then you will be a walking ascended being."

There is a pause.

"Enough of this for now. Let me show you what integration looks like in Gabriel. Hold on." Sam took Gabriel through a series of maneuvers I never thought a helicopter could do—wingovers, barrel rolls and a loop…yes even a loop.

Even though I was not required to demonstrate helicopter acrobatics, I successfully passed my check ride.

XIII

You are a ray of light that does not end,
But goes on and on,
Until it becomes One
With the Source of all Light.

The days flew by, literally, blurred one into another. I enjoyed my talks with Sam and learning about the spiritual journey and what he taught me. As always, he showed me things in the 47 that I never thought possible. Then one day while flying over an Alabama cotton field…

"Robert, ever heard of Shangri-La?"

"You mean Shambhala."

"Maybe, I mean the mythical kingdom in Tibet. I think both names are used … not sure."

"I once read a story about an ancient utopian city in the Himalaya's of Tibet where people live forever. By Hilton, 'Lost Horizon.' They made a movie of it back in the 1930s."

"That's it. What if I were to tell you that it really exists."

"No way! That's pure fiction. Besides how do you know?"

"I've been there."

"Huh? I thought, at best, it was a legend."

"It exists, but it's hidden."

I shook my head in disbelief and focused on getting the right heading for the coast.

Sam continued. "It is an ancient city of light from the fifth dimension placed on earth as a test. The legend was accurate, it was in the Himalayas. At the time, the Himalayas held a portal, and a sacred location, well isolated and protected with a higher vibration."

"fifth dimension?"

We'd talked around that before, but never really got to the core.

"Right. The fifth dimension, as opposed to the 3rd dimension where we are today, is a state of higher consciousness where there is oneness, unity, and love. These same characteristics were seeded into Shangri-La. It was an experiment by the Galactic Federation, like ancient Atlantis, to see if the third dimension could hold a fifth dimensional city of light, and maintain the connection with the Source-of-All."

"So, they imported fifth dimension people for the city… to live on earth."

"That's right."

"Sometimes, Sam, I think we're nuts. But the thought's intriguing. If all this were true, then the inhabitants of Shangri-La were experiencing both the third dimension and fifth dimension at the same time." Sam nodded assent. I went on, "Was the experiment successful? After all, Atlantis was an experiment and it was destroyed."

"Well, this worked a little better. The people of Shangri-La recognized that the duality was an illusion, called it a dream and in the process of recognizing and accepting this they were able to transcend it and find and experience joy, love health and expanded consciousness. But their problem, in the original city, was that it was closed off from the third dimensional world. The experiment worked in that they proved that the earth's energy field could hold them but they had to put it in an isolated, hidden area of the planet to protect them from the earth's lower consciousness and vibrational level at the time. Only certain people of higher vibration were allowed in and very few at that."

"What is it like…this Shangri-La?"

"Well, how about we go and find out."

"What…where?"

Flying With My Higher Self

"There is a duplicate of Shangri-La where we are going. I got the controls."

Before I knew it Sam had Gabriel in a climb. The altimeter registered 1000…2000 feet and we were still climbing.

"Hey Sam…Gabriel has a service ceiling limit." *The manual said it was 10,000 feet. I knew that helicopter performance is very slim at altitude.*

"There are no limits where we are going Robert!" Sam said laughing out loud.

I thought to myself …great…two pilots found frozen like a rock and dead in Alabama from in-flight breakup… 5,000 feet, man… its getting cold in here.

"You still with me Robert?"

"I think so. Do you think it's a smart idea to be…" The altimeter was reading at 9000 feet and climbing.

Sam interrupted. "Just take a few deep breaths …very deep now. Close your eyes and follow my instructions. Ready, we are going to do this together."

My mind was racing - close my eyes? I wondered whether this guy had a death wish he was about to reveal. But I trusted him.

Sam's voice sounded thin and far away. "In your mind's eye, set the intention to see Shangri-La, this beautiful white crystalline city, —don't worry about whether you're there or not —just see the city as best you can. Imagine it and it will be there."

"Got it."

"Okay, good, keep the focus now… you are using your higher thought to project yourself there…so on my count now: three …two…one, project yourself there NOW. You are in Shangri-La."

Suddenly, I was enveloped in a corridor of bright light and felt lighter and freer and rising out of my body.

"What do you see?"

"I can see it and it feels like what I have seen in pictures and read about. There are these enormous snow-covered mountains, glaciers, and steep ravines and valleys. There is a light shining ahead."

"Good, let's head towards it." The helicopter shuddered for a moment, a new odd vibration. It tugged at me but I was caught up in the vision.

"I see a huge entrance shimmering in the light—a giant gate fading in and out..."

"Me, too."

"Can we go in?"

Almost immediately, "Sam...the gate is opening..."

"Good, lets walk in."

Just like in dreams, we were out of Gabriel and standing by an enormous gate. Huge, marble-like structures, out of nowhere, and we were at the top of a rise looking back at a lush green valley. It was beyond anything I imagined.

"Sam...what's going on? God, I feel like I'm in a new body...lighter, freer, hard to describe..." It was like a bubble inside me, lifting, a strange euphoria.

"This is your fifth dimensional body, a replica of the one on earth. It is perfect...no illnesses, disease, negativity...it is pure light made in the image of the creator."

Shoot, I briefly thought to myself, I have a perfect body and I've spent years working on the old one.

"Yes, when you incarnated on the earth plane, you left this, a reminder that you're Spirit and will be returning home after your earth experience. Time is different here."

"What...this fifth dimensional me?"

"It's a higher aspect of yourself suggesting ways of living and being. It's the source of joy, happiness, and creativity. It is the part of you that is your own spirit guide and higher self, Robert."

I pulled my eyes from the incredible perfection before me and looked to Sam. Almost didn't want to speak for fear of losing this moment, but had to. "Sam, without time, without space. Then, I can create by just imagining and it happens."

"Something like that. On earth, we need the time-space construct so we can experience everything: light and dark, creation and consequences. Linear time gives us past, present and future. In the fifth dimension, there is no time, only the present moment, only now."

"Let's fly!" Before I knew it, I was flying in a 47 as Sam's wingman. Wow, no engine start, no takeoff, all at once we were flying and I was on his right side. This was way cool I thought. And, I didn't have to say anything; it was as if I could read Sam's thoughts and he could read mine. So, this is how telepathy works.

We were cruising low in a deep luscious valley surrounded by enormous mountains, Sam on my left and myself tucked in close by. Then, unexpectedly, Sam turned into a snow-capped peak off our nose.

"Sam…dammit… there is a mountain dead ahead. Turn right, NOW!" I hesitated and watched, but something told me to stay with him, so I did.

He kept going, I was on his tail, and I knew we were dead, but we were in a dream weren't we, and then it was all right, we were flying right *through* the mountain. *You can fly through a mountain in the fifth dimension!*

After passing through we came out into another green valley. I looked around and the aircraft was intact. We had just flown through a frickin' mountain!

I could hear Sam in my mind saying, let's do that again and sure enough we were flying through the mountains.

I was closing fast on him. Don't want to lock rotors—sure way to die, I am thinking now. Recklessly, I flew right up to Sam, hesitating at first and then touched his rotors expecting to see debris and pieces of the rotors and fuselage. Nothing happened.

"Here, there's no such thing as collisions Robert. No laws of time-space to worry about here. Don't want to try this on Earth." Sam was laughing in my head.

Suddenly I was flying my 47 next to Sam's as if nothing had happened. Yes, you could fly your helicopter into a mountain and into another aircraft in this world if you wanted to.

"Okay Robert, how about we begin to head back…" I thought…great because I am freezing my butt off.

Sam turned Gabriel westward and we began a gradual descent leaving 12,000 feet and slowly spiraling down to earth. We were both quiet for a few minutes.

"Sam, what the hell happened? That was amazing. I'm either hallucinating from altitude or …"

He looked at me and smiled.

"I can't let it go. How do I embody my fifth dimensional body in the here and now of our third dimensional reality?"

We leveled off and headed north. "Great question. Just know that you are multidimensional, Robert. You exist in many dimensions at once. Science has shown that we can be in two different locations at the same time. And when you dream at night you inhabit a dream body in another dimension."

"Instead of thinking linearly, consider the possibility that things, realities, are more, uh, circular with multiple dimensions interacting and overlapping all at once."

"Back to what you said, or I think you said, earlier …when I'm in fifth dimensional body, I'm really experiencing a perfect image of myself."

"Precisely."

"Man, it felt great. Lighter, freer, limitless, energized, expanded, full of love and joy like I could do or go anywhere—it was unbelievable."

"Now, slip back into this body again, you can bring back all of that, all those qualities –the joy, excitement, expansion and others -- into your third dimensional body."

"Like I'm in my own Shangri-La."

"Yep, that's one way to see it. Your fifth dimensional body has attributes and qualities that far surpass anything typical in this world. For example, you have greater psychic abilities, can see energies, use telepathy, teleportation, healing abilities, space travel and go anywhere in fifth dimension and the galaxy."

"I'm still grappling with what we did earlier. By setting that intention at first, we were able to project our thoughts into the fifth dimension. And could communicate telepathically." I thought for a moment, back in earth-think, damn, that's going to put the radio and telephone companies out of business."

"Thought projection is the ability, which we all have but forget about, to direct your energy, your spirit, to another level and place. You think of a place, no matter what the distance in the universe and you can be there instantly."

"That sounds incredible."

Flying With My Higher Self

"Thought moves faster than light which travels at 186,000 feet per second. We created an inter-dimensional corridor, gateway as we climbed even at our slow speed and with our thoughts we propelled ourselves into the fifth dimension. If you want to go to Jupiter you just think you are there, and you are. Can't do that in a space ship."

"Tower, Zero One, is five miles for landing."

"Zero One, Tower, roger… where have you boys been hiding?"

"Shangri La," Sam said smiling.

"Well, there ain't no town by that name around here sweetheart. Welcome back and glad to hear your voice again. You guys owe me a drink for this. We grew worried when you did not return yesterday, had to report you missing and have had folks out looking for you since."

"Yesterday!"

"Roger, tower, very sorry about that…we were *exploring* the area."

"Roger, understand "area." Well, there is no Area 51 around here if that's what you're referring to. Maybe over a dinner you can share with me what that… Shangri-La place is like, One Zero."

"Uhh, will do tower." Sam turned to me, "I love that woman. Want to do the landing?'

"Of course!"

XIV

Trust the bonds that you have created with others.
Know that the greatest gift that you can give is your friendship.
Your friends are the very souls you have chosen
to journey with in this lifetime. They are an
important part of your growth and learning.

I handed him the rolled-up New York Times. "Not much in there to make you smile, Sam."

"Maybe not – but remember you create your own reality."

"True, but I find myself spending a lot of time listening to the news, surfing the channels.

I want to know what's going on, but most of the time I find it just brings me down. Literally. My vibration, my energy just droops. Just reading the paper does that to me. And the evening news can be worse since it's easy to get caught up in an issue being discussed."

I settled into one of the folding chairs Sam had set up outside the hangar. "A reputed metaphysician, Muktananda, recommended that everyone avoid television, radio and the media as much as possible because of the harm the negative energy can do to our vibrational levels. He was concerned that our subconscious would absorb that pollution."

Sam was looking out into the horizon where the sunset was painting the puffy white clouds pink and purple.

"I suspect that much of what we see in the news is manufactured. Not "fake" the way some critics complain just versions of things that don't, can't, include the whole truth and context. It's so much easier to color things black or white or give a version of a story that is either not true or doesn't include the whole truth." Sam waved the paper at me and said "We could all use a bit more discernment."

I thought for a moment before nodding my assent. "Okay, I agree. That's another thing easier said than done."

"Not so hard really. Just ask yourself, "Is this truth in alignment with me? If not, then *choose* another reality. Also, remember you came to earth to experience the duality…the polarity of this environment. Don't discount that. It's how you *react* that counts."

"Are you saying that I somehow attract the news and its negativity?"

"Yes. You choose to bring it into your awareness."

"So, you are suggesting I choose differently."

"Right. Remember, the news is a snapshot of what's going on collectively in your environment (and not everything I may add). How you perceive it and how you choose to react to it will influence your energy and vibration levels."

"So, if it looks pretty sad and fearful – like the constant war in the Middle East – I'll feel and attract that fear and negativity. The converse is true as well I guess."

"Yeah, the trick is to become aware of your judgments. When a news story comes up, check what you're thinking and feeling. Just be aware of it."

"So, what I perceive happening in the collective is a reflection of what is going on within me."

"That's right. Check in on what comes up for you. For instance, if you feel angry and frustrated with something, ask yourself where you're holding anger and frustration within yourself?"

I leaned back and pondered what he had said. "Take the recent election, there was a lot of anger, frustration, powerlessness and helplessness with the outcome. For many, it was like, how did this happen? And the ramifications were huge. It was downright depressing."

"First, regarding the recent election, it was the collective consciousness that brought that potential future into manifestation."

"Sam, I see your point, but a lot of us were hoping for a different outcome."

Flying With My Higher Self

"True. There was an energy that wanted to manifest a particular outcome—this candidate you speak of and another that did not want it to happen—instead they wanted to manifest a different outcome. What you focus on perpetuates itself energetically. By focusing on and against it the result was guaranteed."

"So, those who voted against him essentially helped him win."

"Remember—it's a YES Universe. The result gave everyone what they focused on, whether it was a positive focus or not. It doesn't discriminate."

I paused for a moment to take this beautiful moment in; the sun was down and cloud's brilliance was fading in the afterglow.

Sam continued, "But since this is the reality now, you have to ask yourself, "Where is this scenario being played out in my life? Where do I feel so powerless? Where do I feel like a victim? Where am I playing this program in other areas of my life? The beauty here is recognizing that you have the opportunity to see the patterns in your life and shift them. That's integration. Another thing. It's also about being transparent, Robert."

"You mean being calm and centered in my own energies and not being buffeted by everyone else's thoughts, feelings and behavior."

"The analogy I would use is that it's the difference between being the pilot in command flying and being on automatic pilot, along for the ride." We watched a small Cessna line up for take-off. "Ever meet a helicopter pilot who blamed his success or failure on the weather or other event? Not many. Pilots have a keen sense of responsibility about what they do—they are the consummate professionals."

"Agree. Some of the best pilots I flew with had a calm, centered demeanor which was their source of confidence and trust."

"I might add, the key is recognizing the thought, belief or pattern in your conscious awareness. Seeing it shifts you into the co-creator level of awareness and away from the victim or perpetrator energy."

"Where there is no judgment."

"Precisely. At the co-creator level, you're in unity consciousness -- a state of awareness where ALL experiences are acceptable and there's no judgment, no good or bad, not one better than another, no competition, nor either/or. There is only 'and' meaning all options are possible and worthy of consideration."

"So, to circle back to where we came in, you're saying that the news is a manifestation of where the collective consciousness is vibrating and that we're not bound to play out or become part of those frequencies. We can hold our own frequency."

"That's right. Remember you're not a victim, unless you choose to be. If others do not wish to awaken, you're not tied to their reality. You can choose another reality for yourself. When you decide to change, you'll create more love, harmony, abundance and expansion in your life, no matter what everyone else is choosing."

"So, at the higher frequencies, there are no victims. Everyone thrives."

"Yes, and one more thing. Oddly enough, not everyone wants to explore the higher frequencies."

"But why not, if that's where everyone thrives. Why choose another reality?"

"Because that's where they are and where they want to be. We've all been there, right? We can only meet them where they are in their personal growth and honor the choice they made as divine beings of light. Hold for them the wisdom that they may choose to see themselves from a higher perspective. Perhaps you holding the higher frequency will empower them to do likewise."

"That's a tough road to walk."

"It's called *evolution*."

"So, the soul chooses these experiences to grow and evolve – but we can ignore what's going on if we want."

"Sure. Remember that even when the outer world looks dark, the light of God shines from within you; an inner light that constantly uplifts and sustains. It illuminates your way forward in creating a new reality. You can then radiate gratitude for the harmony, prosperity and beauty that surrounds you."

Another day done.

Enlightenment is the realization
That there is nowhere to go,
Nothing to do,
And nobody you have to be,
Except exactly where and how you are right now.

XV

"What do you mean by *Ascension Handbook for Masters*?" I leafed through the small book. I'd retrieved it from the manual a few days before and kept meaning to return it to Sam.

I watched him walk around Gabriel doing a FOD walk, for Foreign Object Damage, looking for flight-line debris that could be ingested into the engine and flight components degrading the performance and jeopardizing the safety of the crew. It was standard procedure done by all pilots before flight.

He looked unimpressed as he walked over to me and stretched out his palm. He'd collected a handful of screws, a piece of metal 2-inches long, some rocks, a latch cover and a feather.

"That stuff can kill you," he said, looking at it and shaking his head.

I nodded in agreement. "Reminds me … Got to tell you how we FOD'ed an international airport which had to be shutdown."

"Can't wait to hear about it." He eased himself into the folding chair I'd set up for him.

"I was the last aircraft on a flight of 8 MH-53J helicopters. We were returning to our home base in Florida after participating in a classified joint special operations exercise in El Paso, Texas. It was getting late and, as we approached the refuel stop at Albuquerque International, the weather was deteriorating. Many in the formation were already at minimum fuel and needed to land. Anyway, Albuquerque Approach had us hold to the south of the airport due to the heavy arrival/departure traffic and the worsening weather. Fuel was getting so low that some in the formation were contemplating landing on the mesa."

"After much radio chatter, we were cleared for a straight in to land on runway 35. The formation began its approach to the runway. The runway in use was 8-26 which intersected runway 35. The wind was from the West around 15 knots as we lined up on 35. It was an amazing sight viewing the flight in trail formation lining up and landing on the 7000 foot runway, holding at the intersection of 8-26. As we landed the combination of our rotor wash, weather, and prevailing winds created an enormous sand storm that blew dirt and tumbleweed through the formation and onto the active runway. There was no way we could have foreseen this."

"Suddenly, the whole airport was blanketed in heavy dust and sand. Air traffic control stopped all traffic - ground and air. We were told to sit tight on the runway. The airport had to be closed and there were some very upset controllers. It took over 20 minutes for the dust to settle and, when it did, we saw a complete mess with debris covering the runways. They had a massive problem on their hands that would take some time to clear.

"We contacted the tower and offered to help. The plan we offered was we'd hover taxi up and down the runway letting the rotor wash clear the debris like a giant leaf blower. I remember there was a pause at the other end of the radio and then a very excited controller allowed us to proceed. We air taxied past the American Airline and Delta jets holding in the taxiway, the crew and passengers watching this giant blower clear the runway. We cleared it in less than 10 minutes and after three passes. Needless to say, the controllers were very pleased."

"Great story." He popped open the little cooler that seemed to never empty and handed me a small orange juice.

"Sam," I said, wiping my wet fingers on my jeans, "tell me about the Ascension Handbook."

"Oh, that," he casually remarked looking over at me. "Something you may need to know about. It's the kind of knowledge a Master would need."

"A Master?" I thought to myself, "is that where I'm heading?"

"That's right. Remember, mastery is the ability to keep all aspects of yourself in a clear, consistent and coherent enlightened state. It's about balance and the amount of light and vibratory frequency that you hold."

"But where does the Ascension fit into it?"

"The ascension is about accessing the fifth dimensional energy that is coming to earth. Since the alignment on December 21, 2012, we've passed into a new vibratory reality. These energies are the vehicle for increasing the consciousness and transforming humanity. And if I may add, it's your job as a Master to embrace this."

I laughed. "My job?" I laughed again. "Well, I've had worse. Bottom line, to experience the fifth dimension here and now, I need to tune myself to these frequencies, or energy." I felt a growing excitement; our trip to Shambhala had opened new worlds for me.

"Precisely. It requires that your body, not just the physical, but also the *etheric*, mental, emotional and spiritual dimensions adapt to this new vibratory state. You'll need to develop the skills to receive, process and transmute these energies so you can continue with the ascension process."

"I thought the ascension process was all about increasing one's awareness and consciousness. Processing and transmuting energy is something more." I guess I frowned, maybe like a kid who found out his homework wasn't done.

Sam just chuckled. "Right – but don't worry. I flipped the pages and pointed to a line "It says here: *Ascension is about recognizing that you are the creator of your reality.*"

"Remember we talked about the light body. The ascension is about raising the light within, letting go of the old programming, integrating new codes, and transforming your physical and etheric bodies into a new dimension—the fifth. As you evolve into this dimension, you are creating a new reality for yourself."

"So, I still stay in my 3rd dimension physical body, but at a new awareness level." I felt slightly reassured.

"That's right. The soul is already multidimensional, because your consciousness is coming from a source beyond this earth-bound reality. It's something innate and natural for you to interact with the fifth and the higher dimensions."

I held up my hand. I had to pause for a moment, nothing unusual when talking with Sam on these subjects. I wished he would slow down, even though a lot of what he was saying seemed to resonate with me at a very deep level as if I already knew it but needed to hear it again. I needed to remember.

"So, let me see if I understand. The ascension is an individual process that one works towards, and this changes our energy field, shifting our vibration to a fifth dimensional consciousness."

"That's right, you got it. The paradox of our 3D world is that you can be in both dimensions simultaneously. It's a reminder that you came to earth to explore a polarity environment while being multidimensional. You are experiencing a multi-presence, multi-dimensional consciousness." He smiled, clearly satisfied with his explanation.

"And we do this by transmuting the energies. Please explain this."

"Okay." Sam watched me pick and peal back the label on the now empty juice bottle. "In the ascension process, you take the third-dimensional body, a denser and lower energy, and transmute it by changing it into higher frequency state."

"So, if you are ascended, that is, and can pull in or change to the higher frequency consciousness, are you then a Master?"

"Yes. In the process of ascension, you've achieved personal mastery. You've completed your soul's lessons and uncovered a fifth dimensional state of consciousness."

"But not all Masters are ascended."

"That's correct. In fact, very few are."

I left that alone. Sam got up, put his folded chair just inside the hanger and opened the cockpit door. I followed suit, got in and started checking the instrument panel and wiping the console.

"Remember, you're already a Master and are just here to play in the duality of earth. If you let that sink in then you will have a more enjoyable experience." He chuckled again, yes, Sam was having a good time this morning.

I thought of our flight to Shambhala and the unbelievable feelings of joy, harmony, and the freedom that swept through me. That total and indescribable peace still resonated. I let myself enjoy that moment. "Then by bringing fifth dimension qualities in to the 3rd, this allows me to open up to new possibilities and creations." I knew I was repeating something, like I wanted to inscribe it in myself somehow. "And help others on their paths."

Sam nodded slowly but deliberately, like the slow student had finally gotten the concept. "That's right, and by helping others you fulfill your greater purpose as a star seed by teaching them how to heal themselves and the planet. Your life expands to a higher calling."

I added, "So, when I've completed my reason for being here, learned my soul lessons, and have accepted myself completely, then I can assume that I'll ascend to another level of consciousness."

"Something like that."

I read the next line, *The process of Ascension is not a contest.*

"Ascension is a process, not a destination. It's all about the journey, Robert. Very important. Everyone eventually ascends in his or her own time and way, including the planet. All in divine order." He scanned the horizon.

The ascension process is your birthright.

"You have the codes of ascension within you. They just need to be activated. Ascension is a very personal process between a person and their higher-self. It's something you have contracted with your higher self before you incarnated."

"How do I do that, I mean bring the codes into my awareness?"

"This evening when you meditate, set the intention to tune into the higher energies and transmute the lower ones; strengthen your energy field and use your meditations, chanting and other tools to raise your light quotient and vibration."

"It says here that *All make the journey of Ascension; Shine your light to those following behind you...*"

"The notion that everyone ascends suggests that there are different waves or iterations of the ascension. But it is inevitable."

Sam looked at me and smiled. "Yes. All ascend in their own time. Those that ascend first leave the gift of light energy to those behind them. In fact, many of those left behind are star seeds, like you, who've volunteered to remain and help others on their journey."

"Sam, do I need to prepare for the ascension? Do something different or more?"

"As they say, 'keep on keeping on.' Continue what you're doing now, Robert, for your spiritual journey IS the process through which you activate your ascension codes. It's all about increasing awareness and consciousness. It's not about pushing or striving for a specific outcome. Instead proceed with trust, love and joy."

I looked at Sam, "Sam, you sure are an impressive guy, knowing all this stuff."

"So, do you, of course. I just know that I know all these things." He laughed at the confidence of the statement, and reached for the pre-flight checklist.

XVI

I remember showing up at the airport cafeteria, our typical meeting place, eager to talk with Sam. I had the strangest dream the night before; I dreamed that I wouldn't see him again. It left me unsettled. It recalled the first dream I had after we met where we had been flying together and he had suddenly disappeared. Perhaps it was a ghostly premonition. But this one felt like a final good-bye and it left me troubled and sad.

We usually met around 10:00 am, looked at the weather, and decided then if we would fly or not. I ordered two coffees and the bagels. Whether we flew or not, I looked forward to our time together. I took out the handbook and just flipped the pages, opening to: *No one dies at a time or in a way that is not of their choosing.*

Well, that's reassuring, I guess. I wasn't sure I understood the meaning but it suggested that we know beforehand when we're going to die; almost a predestined outcome. Later, I'd realize that these words from the handbook were the only warning I had. Then I heard Sam's voice behind me.

"No one dies before their time."

"Sam?" I turned to see him looking at me with his piecing brown eyes. He was wearing his ballcap with Gabriel's picture on it. He didn't look well--gaunt, his face was ashen white. He slowly sat down across from me and took his cap off placing it gently on the table. Maybe I just hadn't seen it before.

"There's continuity of life Robert, nothing dies. The soul—higher self sees a death experience as a transition into another body, call it the light body, as a formality. You turn one suit in for another. Close your eyes in one dimension; open them again in the next."

I smiled at him and said, "It's how the game is played, right?"

He nodded.

"Sam, you don't look well. What's going on?"

"Thanks for your kind concern, Robert. Been a rough couple of days, but this will soon pass."

"Have you seen a doctor? I could drive you over."

"Already been."

"Well?"

"They're running tests, should have results in a few days."

"What kind of tests?"

"MRI…CT scan, blood work, you know what doctors do…"

I grew quiet. I wasn't at all sure that this was time, but took a chance. I told him about my dream. "It felt as if I was going to never see you again."

"That's not possible."

"I just had this feeling."

He gently put his hand on my hand. "Life happens my friend."

"Yes, of course."

Looking at me intently, he leaned back in his chair and said, "We are always connected, Robert, don't forget that, Okay?"

"You know you have said this to me before, and sure I feel it…but…"

"Do you doubt it?"

"Well, no but…it hasn't been easy, you know…" I couldn't find words.

"Didn't you ask your higher self *What can I share with the world?*"

"Why… yes,"

"What was your answer?"

"Something like…why don't you tell them about US?"

"That's right…US!"

"So here we are…US, Robert and Sam."

I looked at him with a smile. "It was you all along, wasn't it?"

"Right."

"By the way that was brilliant." I said,

"What?"
"The dream about the helicopter pilot and the lost city…"
He chortled then smiled "Got your attention, didn't it?"
I grinned in reply.
"Found yourself in it, did you not?"
"Yes, I did."
"I logged some hours trying to get people to go to the City," Sam was chuckling, "that is until YOU came along."
"Tell me about the girlfriend in your story." I asked smiling.
"Oh, yeah…had to dump her. Best for us both," Sam's chuckle softened and stopped.
"So, what was the point?"
"Some people think they know everything!"
"You mean by trusting their higher self?"
"Not trusting. But you did."
He smiled, looking at me with those warm, deep-penetrating brown eyes.
"I recall a famous Master that came to earth and used to tell lots of stories…parables. You said something about wanting an ascended master or highly evolved being as you worded it, to come 'down' to earth from some imagined heavenly realm…"
"Right, something like that."
"And, if you are still wondering, the helicopter pilot looking for the City of Light was YOU listening to your higher self, trusting and following it despite the impossibilities. And… the guy you picked up was also *you*. When you found the City, you were transformed with a renewed sense of purpose--and all you wanted to do was share it with others. And, as you found out, not everyone shared your desire and excitement. It later becomes your life work--helping others, like yourself, to awaken to the higher aspects of themselves."
"It was YOU all along, wasn't it?"
"And you never doubted that did you…"
"I suspected it, of course."
"Well… who do you think was helping you write this story, after all?"
"Of course."

"And you experienced a miracle."

"You mean you coming here?"

"Perhaps, and the remembering."

"Remembering?"

Sam smiled, "The answer to the arrival of the ascended master as you called it."

"That you were to find out something about yourself…"

Sam continued, "…and that the answers to all your questions were and had always been within you; co-creating the life I want with my higher self and that is *how the game is played*!"

I smiled at him as I sipped my coffee.

Sam began coughing and then reached for the glass of water. "I rest my case."

"Sam…promise me something."

Sam hesitated and looked up, "Shoot."

"You'll be with me forever."

He smiled and said "Always have been, Robert, always will be. Let's face it… there's no letting go."

XVII

In the path of your happiness, find the learning
for which you have chosen this lifetime.

That morning, Sam and I had our last flight together. We didn't talk much. We didn't have to. Everything had already been said. As far as he was concerned, he'd answered my call and I was grateful. I did not want it to be over, though. But there was still one nagging question that lingered in my mind.

"Sam, you never told me how you became my Higher Self."

"Thought you'd never ask." He glanced over at me, "Are you ready?"

"Yeah, sure."

"Here's the short version. Give you the longer version in our next life together. Before your Soul came into being in the Universe, Robert, I was a sixth dimensional being from star system Arcturius. Arcturians reside primarily between the fifth and sixth dimensions. I was a starship commander, with the mission to patrol a sector of your galaxy under the Command of Sanat Kumura. It was a great job, very demanding and also very rewarding. Anyway, after fulfilling those responsibilities, the Galactic Federation offered me the chance to focus in the fourth and fifth dimension and help star seeds like yourself evolve. That's how we came together. We've been together for a very long time, my dear friend and it has been the most rewarding and precious experience for me."

I was deeply moved by what he had just shared.

"But I am getting ahead of myself. A very long time before US, on one of my many trips near earth as a Starship commander, I landed my shuttle, really a smaller version of the starship, on earth at a spot not far from here." He stopped to gather his words. "It was on that trip that I met and fell in love with a most extraordinary woman. Today, you'd call her a shaman and planetary healer. She was a very advanced being herself, able to travel through the interdimensional worlds. I was on the fifth dimension and she was on the third, but due to her extraordinary abilities, she shifted her identity into her Fifth Dimension Light Body. Oh, the things we shared."

He lifted the glass of water to his lips.

"But my duties as starship commander required me elsewhere and I had to leave. We've stayed in communion with each other in other dimensions, even though we are generally physically separated.

"Her Arcturian name is Elaine, and my love for her has spanned hundreds of thousands of earth years."

"It's Jan, right?"

"Yes."

"Why didn't you tell me?" I asked surprised.

"Because it would have distracted me from my mission which was to be with you. You surely can see that we Arcturians are very mission oriented."

"Yes, but…"

"Jan and I have been able to see each other a lot in this lifetime, Robert, and during this visit. I'm very grateful for this. It's been an unexpected gift."

"I am glad this happened, Sam." The truth struck me and I looked at him, "But…you're leaving again."

"If you are concerned about Jan, no need to worry. She understands."

"What is Jan's role now?"

"She, too, is from Arcturius and an ascended Master who's returned to earth again to help guide others on their ascension journey. She's a beautiful soul, Robert."

"Sam, is there anything I can do?"

"Yes. You need to meet her."

"Yes, of course. Sam. Another thing. And this sounds selfish, I know, but I'd love for you to show me around one of those Arcturian starships. Is that possible?"

Sam's face lit up at the suggestion. "That can be arranged, my friend."

We refueled and flew some more in the afternoon. Sam told me jokingly that he was cashing in all his earth frequent flyer miles and getting what he could in the third dimension, before departing. He shared that despite its challenges, he liked being in the third dimension and especially flying Gabriel. We flew over Jan's home like we did on our first flight, then took turns chasing and flying through clouds like a couple of kids. He continued to amaze me with the things he would do with Gabriel.

He died peacefully a few days later. He said he was ready. I was blessed with the opportunity to perform a healing by his bedside before he died. It was a very intimate moment for both of us. He showed me how to die to self with grace and dignity. His last words to me were that it been a 'good run' and that he was glad to 'be moving on', and 'going home.'" More than anything he said that he enjoyed the opportunity to honor my request. He had a last wish—he wanted his ashes scattered from Gabriel over the land he'd grown to love.

XVIII

*Begin to expect the unexpected and embrace the magic
within all of your day-to-day experiences.
Many small yet wonderful surprises are coming your way.
It is the calling of the universe to return to the child-like wonder
and belief that anything can happen.
There is a great amount of love and support available to you.*

It was a grey and windy morning, which matched my mood. I sat staring at my laptop computer in the airport cafeteria, writing about my brief time with Sam, when I heard my name called.

"Robert."

I looked up. Standing in front of me was a petite, middle-aged woman with short blond hair and lovely hazel eyes. I was struck by her calm radiance and beautiful smile.

I rose up from my chair, "You must be Jan."

"Yes, how did you know?" she sounded pleased, extending her hand and grasping mine in a firm handshake.

"I've…heard so much about you. It is so nice to meet you."

We looked at each other, then embraced and held each other for a long time. I finally released her.

As we sat down I asked "How are you doing, after…?"

"I am doing okay, thank you." I could sense that she had been through a rough time with Sam's death.

She reached into her purse and took out an envelope. "I heard a lot about you, Robert. Sam talked about you a lot."

I smiled, looking into her beautiful eyes. She went on,

"Before I forget, Sam asked me to give this to you." She handed the envelope to me.

I took the letter in my hand and just looked at it. "Thank you Jan, is there anything that I can do for you?" I asked.

"You're very kind to ask. Yes. If it's not a burden for you, I would love to learn to fly a helicopter. Sam always talked about teaching me someday."

"Sure. That can be arranged."

"Also, I'd like to get to know you, Robert. I know that sounds odd, but perhaps you understand. There's more that we need to do together.

I smiled. Sam was still with me.

"Of course."

That night I opened the letter addressed to me from Sam.

Dear Robert,

It has been a pleasure sharing this journey with you. I am very proud of who you are, who you're becoming and the life that you are living. Remember me as a part of you—the essence of who you are. I am you and you are me. I am with you always, guiding you and loving you.

I've been with you forever, through all your past lifetimes, reminding you that you have all the answers within you. You have all the inner wisdom about what to do and when to do it. Realize that, as the Son of God, you are already perfect - that whatever you are doing right now is perfect for you; stop striving and trying to be perfect. Everything you are already doing is perfect. Let go of any judgments you have what you ought to be doing to grow spiritually.

Just love yourself and where you are right now. Relax and take a deep breath. Call Light to yourself and surround yourself with it. This is who you are!

You are the pilot of your life—don't forget that. And you're a pretty good one, if I may say so. Another thing. Always remember you are not flying alone… I am always there when you need me. Call on me anytime. We are flying together in eternity!
Sam
PS: Take good care of Gabriel for me! You two are always in my heart.

After reading and pondering the letter, I opened the manual.

The illusion of death as duality comes together into one infinite life.

Don't be dismayed by good-byes. A farewell is necessary before you can meet again. Meeting again, after moments or lifetimes, is certain for those who are friends.

XIX

Spiritual growth is the process of becoming your higher self.
Believe you are a master and you are.

The days after Sam's death were quiet and somber. I felt raw, down and lost in a fog contemplating the shock of it all. There was regret and the guilt of not catching his deteriorating condition earlier, not that I thought I could have changed the outcome. It just felt so sudden and final, just like his appearance at the air show the day we met for the first time. Yet, here I was mourning my dear friend's loss while also reminding myself that I hadn't lost anything or anyone; that Sam was with me and always had been and would be. We were One, inseparable. It was a reassuring thought, yet this truth had not sunk in despite the letter.

I opened the handbook:

You don't die; death is an illusion and not an eternal state of being or a resting place

Okay. Thank you. I get it. I thought to myself, sure death is an illusion. But one so natural to fear. I really missed him.

As I slowly walked out to the flight-line, I saw Gabriel—her white fuselage glowing in the sunlight poised for flight. I wondered if she knew about Sam; consciousness is consciousness and we are all One, I thought. She probably knows, at some level.

Today was going to be my first flight without Sam. It felt strange. As I walked around doing the preflight I'd occasionally catch glimpses of a shadow that seemed to fade in and out as if he was with me, like old times. Now, he likes to show up in my thoughts, something about knowing each other's thoughts without using words, he would say, as Masters do.

It was the typical sort of summer morning that I loved—the hues of red and crimson as the sun rose. I could see the cumulus forming on the horizon, clouds slowly gathering up. Slight breeze. It was going to be a scorcher. Good flying weather I thought.

Hey Gabe…you know what's going on, don't you? The water droplets on the windshield reminded me of tears as if it knew, too, that things were not the same anymore. *We are much better having known him wouldn't you say?* I rubbed my hand over the golden letters stenciled on the tank.

He will be missed…it's you and me now, my friend…hope that's okay.

I strapped myself in the left seat and put on my helmet. Flying with Sam had been a once-in-a lifetime adventure for me, now overshadowed by a strange uneasiness as I sat in his place. My adventure had been about Sam and our conversations, the impossible way he made Gabriel fly and what he taught me. I glanced down at the white box holding Sam's ashes next to me.

Sam…how are you doing, pal?

Hey Robert. The third dimension is hard, takes a little getting used to--want to get beyond time and space…if you know what I mean. Besides, it is more fun here!

Sure, I understand, but…

Hey, glad we were together. Let's keep the conversation going. In fact, what we have shared might make a good book.

Yes, I know…well…thanks for everything.

You are welcome, my friend.

I ran through the start-up checklist and paused momentarily feeling the controls, listening to the hum of the Lycoming engine and twirling of the blades. Oil pressure, fuel flow, engine revolution, rotor speed, manifold pressure, all good. I love those sounds, the feeling of the power. Felt that way in the big Sikorsky too. It felt as if I was coming alive again—a rebirth—hard to explain, but things were changing in my life.

Flying With My Higher Self

Believe you are a master and you are!
Is that you again Sam?
Hello, Master or should I call you Messiah!
Hey, cut it out. Where are you going to drop me?
Where do you want to go?
Not to worry.
Do me a favor...stop by and see Jan when you can.
I will...promise. We have an agreement. Anything you want me to tell her?
Well, that I am okay...not to worry and I'll see her again. That's it. She already knows!
Okay, I'll pass it along.
Oh...take good care of Gabe for me, too...in case you don't know already, she likes it when you talk to her.
Of course. Anything else?
Then silence.
"Tower Gabriel One Zero for takeoff."
"Roger One Zero...flying solo today?"
"Yes...looks like this is it from now on Rita."
"Roger, One Zero you make sure you say hello to Sam for me, okay."
"Wilco...Sam is no...I will..."
"I heard and I'm so sorry...I loved that man...tell you about it one day. Gabriel One Zero cleared for takeoff report clear, winds 180/5knots. You take care now and have a good day, ya hear."
"Roger, Gabriel One Zero"

I headed south at 500 feet glad once more to see the green countryside, the vast, open farmland and luscious fields and stripes of trees that stretched for miles all around. I had been flying for over 20 minutes when I heard, *COME LEFT!* I made an immediate standard left turn.

Roll out! Here it is!
What?
Where I want you to drop me!

I looked around and below and all I could see were flat fields of corn and tree lines. Off to the side was a farmer's dirt road.

Where?
A little further up.
Okay, I get it…what's so special about this place, Sam?
It's where I was reborn, Robert.
Remind me to ask about this.

I dropped Gabe down to 300 feet

Okay…how you would like me to do this?
Come a little left and it will be right off the nose for about 2 miles.

I began a slight left turn.

What am I looking for?
See that large oak tree up ahead? You can't miss it.

Sure enough, right off the nose was a massive old oak alone in the middle of a field of yellow grass.

Okay, I believe I've got it!
Good, wind is off the nose. Slow her down a bit looking for 20 knots groundspeed.
Add a little left pedal.
Good job…Drop at 150 feet, same heading and 20 knots, any faster and you'll be eating me for breakfast. You are okay for a low pass and drop!
Got it!
Ready?

I placed the box of ashes in my lap, holding the cyclic with my right hand and grabbing underneath the box with my left while adding a little left pedal as Sam instructed. As I approached the site I couldn't help but feel the sadness come over me. I concentrated on holding the box steady and gently guided Gabe over the tree.

Bye Sam!

The ashes slowly flew into the breeze as I accelerated and came around for another flyover.

Nice job. By the way, not a bad way to go Robert!
Meaning?
Us Spirits like to fly, if you get my drift.

I supposed he meant the scattering of ashes.

I get it.

As I flew over it again I asked, *So, what's the story with the tree?*

Jan and I spent some time there. It was where we used to meet…where I fell in love again. When you get some time do go there. It's an energetic portal—wonderful energy.

I will.

On the return flight, I recalled a time of scattering the ashes of a fallen airman from my squadron over a wilderness area in New Mexico that he'd loved. An avid outdoorsman, he used to hunt and camp there with his family. His final request was to be scattered over the forest. It was one of the most memorable flying moments of my career.

Thank you, Sam!

XX

Everyone is on a spiritual path. Only some are aware of it.

As the summer flew by, I could sense the changes; the wisps of cooler air, especially in the mornings, and eventually the leaves changing colors. I was feeling more confident and in the flow again. Not as many people came out for rides when the tourists left and the kids went back to school; perhaps an occasional passenger or two. I still enjoyed giving the rides and got a kick out of introducing folks to the thrill of flying in a helicopter.

I've met all kinds of wonderful people. Had a fighter pilot one morning who told me that he heard that flying a helicopter was 'a piece of cake.' He just had to try it to prove something to his oversized ego. Found out it was a little trickier than he expected, especially trying to land. I still laugh remembering the look on his face bringing Gabe in to hover and realizing he had no airspeed instead of the usual 150 + knots. I'm glad to say he enjoyed his morning and walked away with a little humility.

Occasionally, there's a face in the crowd, perhaps a lovely young woman, who makes me want to stay and talk for a while. Or an older man or couple who look familiar, although I'm sure we haven't met. I often wonder if perhaps these encounters suggest we are from the same soul or star seed group and are meant to meet in this life. I'm more open to synchronicities now.

One quiet afternoon without passengers, I took Gabe for a spin. *Okay Gabe, let's have some fun.* I brought her down to tree top level and we screamed over the trees as fast as she would go. Such a pretty land, I thought, and how lucky I am to be doing this. It's the freedom, like setting myself free from all the cares —the routine, boredom and things that tie us down. And, I imagined all this!

I thought about what Sam had said, *It's all about awakening to your mastery…*

Believe you are a master and you are! The words kept ringing in my ears.

I feel at times as if I have not 'mastered' anything, still learning with a long way to go. Never thought of myself as a master. Maybe it's the word 'Master' that rings hollow and sounds boastful.

That isn't where you are, Robert, okay. You are way beyond that. But, if that's where you believe you are then that's fine.

Okay Sam… I am going to check my attitude around this Mastery thing.

It is called acceptance!

Easy for you to say. The whole thing just feels a bit scripted, overused or a cliche to me, perhaps a bit arrogant.

Arrogant! Not at all, because mastery transcends ego. You do not have to prove anything to yourself or anyone else for that matter. Mastery is about awakening to SELF and recognizing and ACCEPTING that you ARE your Higher Self and believing it. Then you are there.

Okay, Okay, I get it!

You and I, as your higher self, are always connected—have been and always will be. It is not about becoming something or reconnecting with me. We're already there. And, it's not about striving either!

I smiled, *Roger that, and thanks for the reminder.*

You are welcome, my friend.

So, we chose to come here… together, US… into form and created illusions of separation in the form of ego and personality to explore duality in the third dimension…again.

It was your choice to incarnate, with a little help, of course.

So, all of this is an illusion that we created along with all the motions, thoughts, feelings about being separate and feelings of not being good enough and not connecting; to explore duality.

Precisely. Just think of it as a dream. Masters know that the earth is a purposed illusion-a special university chosen to learn responsible creation.

I added, "We're never ever separate from Source energy -- just having a good time in our earth experience."

Right! Play your 365 roles each year with an inward smile and with the remembrance that you are only dreaming. Great consolation comes from the realization that 'I AM Spirit'. Hey, let's fly through those clouds up ahead—I love clouds. Ever tell you about the time I ran Gabriel through a storm cloud...

No, what happened?

I made the cloud disappear. It was fun.

Can I do that?

Sure. Try it sometime.

Sam, tell me about the qualities of masters.

I will, but you have to promise me something.

What?

That you will say to yourself, 'I am a Master' and believe it, because you already are.

I am a Master, I am a Master, I am a Master!

Good. Now, Masters do not seek God or the Creator in the heavens or some faraway place outside of themselves—they don't have time for that (chuckling); instead they know that the Creator resides within their heart. The heart is the operating system that Masters use, like your Windows computer system. They trust their inner messages and take action on them.

So, the process of becoming my higher self is the key to becoming a Master.

That's right.

Masters release old programming and beliefs that no longer serve them. They clear out the rubbish to bring more balance and harmony in their minds and emotions. They recognize that fear and separation create pain and contract their energy. Release the old to bring in the new.

Masters are explorers of self. They accept themselves on ALL levels of their being and are willing to open and surrender to everything good they know themselves to be. They don't mind showing their authenticity and vulnerability!

Masters show unconditional love to themselves and use that love to heal themselves and others. They accept the love and power within their being as their truth.

Masters are a radiating source of light and build their Light Body. They keep their Light Body in a coherent, clear, and enlightened state to gain higher states of consciousness. As they grow spiritually they become their higher self, and help others to find the light. Their high vibration raises all of humanity.

Masters attract a community of supportive, positive people and empower themselves and others in all they do.

Masters know who they are, why they are here, and what their higher purpose is.

Masters co-create with the Source of All their reality. They manifest the reality they want to experience.

Like making dark clouds disappear!

You got it!

Masters acknowledge with gratitude and humility how far they have already come and affirm a commitment to a higher purpose and service to others and the world.

Masters know that 'the truth of being in the world but not of it' is something they must learn and apply. Masters operate with love as the highest expression of who they are.

That was awesome.

Thank you. It is your job now to be a master BY ACCEPTING THAT YOU ARE ALREADY A MASTER!

How does this being a Master translate into practicality? I asked.

Continue to do what you are doing, for Spirit is showing you the way. Strive less, observe more, allow, don't be impatient with yourself and have FUN. Let me repeat that. HAVE FUN! Okay. You are not here to struggle and suffer. Be gentle with yourself and just BE. Stay balanced and in the flow, connected to Source. Feel the rhythm of your life through your heart and love more. Live and love from the Heart. Enough said!

I scanned the instruments watching the clouds boiling up towards the South, a prelude to the summer afternoon thunderstorms. I thought about how pilots know how to become one with their machines; they know them as a part of themselves, a very special and unique bond. That Oneness that is talked about in metaphysical circles, pilots already know. Sam used to say that Gabe is the one flying; he (Sam) just points it in the right direction.

Flying With My Higher Self

And then out of nowhere…
Do you remember the picture?
Picture?
The one you drew on the back of the ship's stationary paper.
Ship's stationary? It took me a moment to gather my thoughts.
Oh yeah, it was aboard the U.S.S. Nimitz, September 21,1985. We were on a highly sensitive operation to penetrate a country in the Middle East to rescue six American hostages held by the Islamic Jihad terrorist group. I was part of the special operations package deployed for the recovery.
What was significant about the picture, Robert?
I had drawn the entire operation, prior to the mission going down. It showed the helicopter in the landing zone surrounded by the SOF assault team's protective perimeter. The hostages were being led onto the helicopter and the airborne cover was flying overhead in support. Still have that picture somewhere in my attic.

Rescue Operation

Yes, you planned and created an outcome. The operation went down just as you drew it. Remember the words you wrote on top?

Yeah, ...they were from scripture, book of Isaiah. "Who will I send, who will go for us?" I said, "Here I am send me"

So, what's this all about Sam?

You were given that quotation from Isaiah. You were saying to Spirit, here I AM—use me.

Up in my attic, somewhere, is the old newspaper article reprint:

Rev. Weir, 61, a Presbyterian missionary, was released Saturday after 16 months of captivity and handed over to U.S. officials in Beirut, White House spokesman Edward Djerejian said.

The New York Times reported Thursday that Rev. Weir carried a message from his captors laying out demands for the release of the remaining Americans held captive. A senior administration official declined to specify the contents of the message but was quoted as saying it was essentially a restatement of earlier demands. There are no new conditions for the release of the hostages that we're aware of," the Times quoted the official as saying.

Rev. Weir's release and his mysterious trip to rejoin his family in Norfolk, Va., were kept secret because ``we were concerned that making it public would interfere with what we hoped would be the imminent release of the other six hostages,`` Djerejian said.

Yep, we got him and the others were eventually released.

Your picture and quote were the light beam illuminating the path. You were a Master and probably never realized it! He was right. Yes, the result was surprising, considering the original plan was a direct assault on the camp which never materialized.

What about the flight in?

We flew through the city, low and fast at night for the pick-up. It worked flawlessly, and as planned.

Sam continued…But another even more desirable outcome developed. All the hostages were released. A combination of factors were at work in your favor beyond your control and the plan changed abruptly. What you had drawn was the best possible future that manifested, as you desired setting the stage for a future positive outcome. That's how mastery works!

Definitely another perspective which had eluded me, in particular the turn of events during that operation. Made me think of others we did.

1978… in the desert in 29 Palms California, I was going to hit the ground—did not have the power to fly—too heavy. There was…

Sam's voice cut in. *…an updraft. Lifted the CH-53A.*

Could not believe how lucky we were. We were resigned…

To crash…you heard, when I spoke.

I never understood what happened. It was a real hot day over 114. I was a new helicopter aircraft commander. We loaded all 26 Marines and I was not able to get through trans lift before we began settling to the ground. The rotor speed was dropping from 100…95 …90…85…82…80 and nothing flies below that according to manufacturer. Then for some unexplained reason we climbed out as the airspeed and rotor speed slowly began to rise again. It felt like an eternity Sam, but we made it.

Hey sport, when things go wrong you have a tendency to call us in.

I don't remember calling anyone Sam—I was bracing for ground impact.

If I recall you said. "Shit… God help us!"

What?

Gave you a second or two to do something about it then I kicked in with a little updraft. Apparently, God had other plans for you (chuckling).

I started laughing, remembering all the other close calls and wondering about all the help I had received throughout my flying career. And very grateful, of course.

Sam. Hold on…. I've got a problem here. There's a split in engine rpm. Something's not right. I heard the engine coughing and turned right towards the airfield monitoring the gauges. All were in the green.

ROLL OUT NOW…the field's straight ahead.

YES!
Start the autorotation early!
I did that just as the rpm rolled down on the gages and the engine seized.
60 knots...looking for sight...only see trees. Oh shit... power lines ahead.
You've got it. Keep speed at 60 till 100 feet—It'll clear the wires.
My chest tightened. SHIT Sam ... GOING RIGHT FOR THE WIRES. At 100 feet, I flared, barely clearing the trees and power lines by five feet. Coming up on 20/20...ten feet, pulling full up collective...touchdown. Just like the practices.
Thanks Sam...there weren't many landing sites.
Nice job. You would have seen it.
Just like the old days Robert!

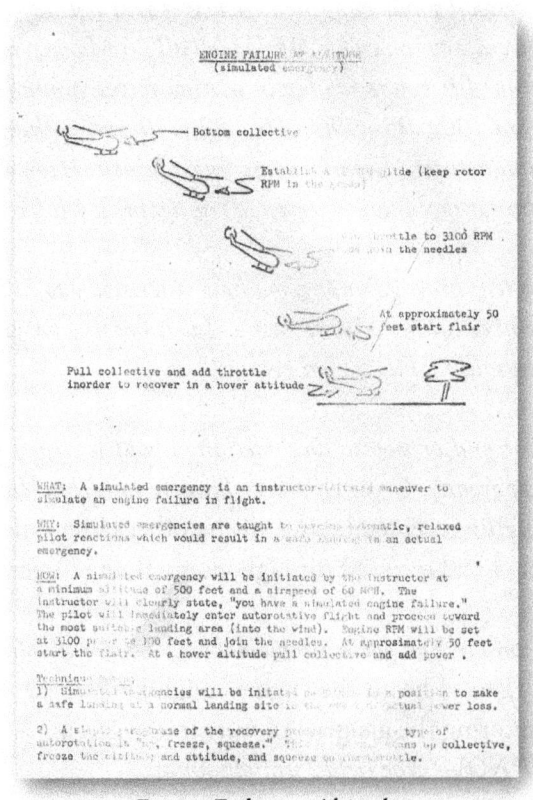

Engine Failure at Altitude

Flying With My Higher Self

Old Days? Is that supposed to make me feel better?
Looks like an oil pressure line. Got your tool box handy?

Go where you want to go, do what you want to do. Be open to all possibilities, and you will own your future.

XXI

You become what you dream!

A few months later, I'm offering rides at the local airport. I've rented some space in a small hangar. Folks around here can't get enough of 'Gabe,' she steals the show every time. I suspect they like the thrill of flying in helicopters, and perhaps are curious how something like it can fly. The airport manager likes having us around; says it brings in more business and tourists to the area.

The sign in front of Gabriel said it all: "Change Your Life and See the City of Light. Donations accepted." Some ask what it's like to fly a helicopter, others just look at the sign, and turn away, some smiling and some shaking their heads. A few just want to talk; I hope they feel better afterwards. Of course, a number will ask, "What is this City of Light?" I'll explain it as a metaphor for life and the spiritual journey. You never know where those conversations will lead.

A very talkative elderly woman once asked, "Are you a flying pastor or something...like the TV show... the Flying Nun?" I had to tell her that I was not a preacher but I really enjoyed the show growing up. She laughed and walked away.

I remember a boy, maybe ten years old, coming up, dragging his mom along, asking for a ride. His mom said he had seen us fly over their house and each time her son would run out all excited, pointing at the helicopter. Used to do that as a kid too. Awfully young, but he looked alert and ready.

I said sure and after helping him into the cockpit and adjusting the helmet and straps, we started up Gabriel and were off. After landing, he jumped out and ran to his mother excitedly telling her all about it. Those were the very rewarding flights.

Then one morning, as I was washing Gabriel outside the hangar, a young man approached me and in a nonchalant voice that I thought I recognized said, "Hello Robert."

"Sam…" I dropped the hose to the ground and turned to see a man, about twenty, maybe six feet tall, long brown hair braided at the back, jeans and a broad smile on his face.

"Sorry. Do I know you?" I asked wiping off my hands.

He smiled and said, "I think so."

"Well…Mr…How can I help you?"

"Jerry…Jerry Whitehouse."

"Nice to meet you again, I guess, Jerry."

"I understand that you offer rides and flying lessons."

"That's right. Are you interested?"

"Maybe, I heard great things about you from a mutual acquaintance…a Sam Watson?"

Startled I asked, "How do you know Sam?"

"We met some time ago, a few years back. Lost track of him sorry to say."

"Well, Jerry, Sam is no longer with us. He just passed a few months ago."

"I know."

He looked at me for the longest time. "Sam was right."

"Right about what?' I asked slightly annoyed at the ambiguity of the whole exchange.

"About you and where I'd find you."

I looked at him seriously, curious now, and ready for anything. "So, Jerry are you really here for the flying, or do you have something else in mind?"

As I was to find out many flights later, the answer to my question was staring at me all along. I began meeting people like him who were, in some strange way, meant to enrich each other's life. Call it synchronicity, coincidence, whatever. I had the feeling Sam had something to do with this.

Flying With My Higher Self

Jerry and I stayed in touch and became good friends. When he married his high school sweetheart in North Carolina, I was his best man. Jerry had just finished flight school at that time and now he's pursuing a military career flying for the U.S. Marine Corps. Another coincidence? Maybe.

XXII

Masters always choose their tests!

I missed Sam, yet knew he was still with me. I picked up the booklet that had been tucked into the back cover of the Bell 47 Flight Manual, *Reminders for the God-Fearing Helicopter Pilot on the Spiritual Path*. Sam had handwritten it. There was a note for me inside, although he had written it before I met him at the airport that first day.

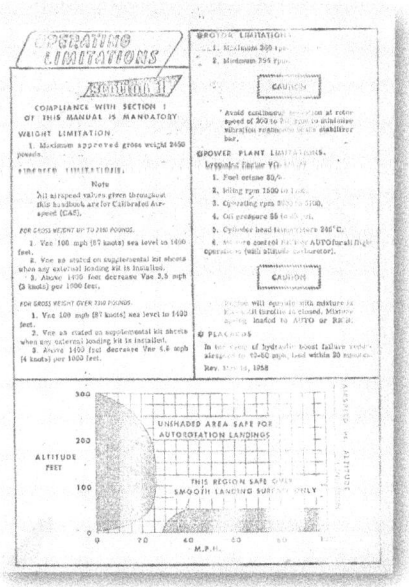

Operating Limitations

"Robert, share this with your students on their journey toward self-mastery."

I. <u>Inspect your aircraft carefully before each flight</u>.

    Helicopter pilots, especially, must do a thorough preflight. He/she is ultimately responsible for safety and it starts here. Take time to inspect and check everything; it's a prudent habit. I've found 'foreign objects' like lose fasteners, even tools, in or near flight controls, and leaks indicating more serious issues during preflight. Remember the bird nest snuggled in the fuel tank.

    <u>Spiritual application</u>: Before embarking on your spiritual path, check your inner pilot, your attitude, commitment and motivation—to see where you are. This may require some reflection on your life purpose and goals. Some tried and true questions: What am I all about? What's my purpose? Why am I here? What in me is resisting this? How committed am I to this path and changing my life? You may be unsure you want to do this, and this is understandable. You may already have a mask or idealized image of yourself in place to help you avoid addressing your flaws and imperfections. Or you may be already on a different journey that doesn't include an obvious spiritual component. That's okay. Many of us do not realize that we are on some sort of spiritual journey. Our level of commitment may be related to our chosen vocation.

II. <u>Make sure you have enough fuel</u>.

    Don't only check the fuel gauges and the fuel tanks on preflight, but also consider having a reserve, just in case. Most pilots know that Murphy's law tends to make most flights longer than planned so the best way to guard against the inevitable is to add fuel.

    <u>Spiritual application</u>: What resources do I bring to the path? You may ask; Do I know who I am? What are my strengths and weaknesses and what qualities do I bring to the table? Spiritual "fuel" includes all the resources that will help on your journey and help you progress despite the obstacles—and there will be many. It's not just our own gifts and talents. Look for support from others, spiritual

guides, activities that nourish your soul and build your connection with Spirit.

III. <u>Use extra caution operating on or near the ground.</u>

Helicopters, unlike airplanes, spend a great deal of their time in close proximity to the ground and in hazardous environments which airplane pilots would consider unsafe. The very nature of your mission and flight profile exposes you to more dangers. Be extra vigilant. And watch out for the incredible power from the rotors' downwash (a minor hurricane) which blows up quite a storm close to the ground.

<u>Spiritual application</u>: Slow down and be aware of your surroundings. Cultivate an inner awareness through spiritual practices like meditation, contemplation, and journaling. Pay extra attention to what is going on within you and around you. Be in the now and presence everything. Become enchanted like a child. Be gentle with yourself. You are one of God's creatures. Also, be aware of the effects that you are having on others (your rotorwash). Be kind, considerate, and patient.

IV. <u>Avoid low rpm and always keep it within safe operating range.</u>

Helicopter pilots know that the one thing that will kill them fastest is low rotor rpm. If the main rotor doesn't spin fast enough you won't get enough lift to fly. Helicopter pilots regularly practice 'auto-rotations', a maneuver to save your life and aircraft in case power is lost. It's basically an adrenaline-filled 'glide' to a flare and (one hopes) landing. High rpm above the limit is also dangerous. In turbine powered helicopters the engine fuel control will normally keep the rotor rpm within limits.

<u>Spiritual application</u>: Maintain balance and avoid extremes. Trust your higher self to help restore the inner peace and harmony that allows true awareness and spiritual growth. Helicopter components, like rotor blades, are delicately balanced to perform efficiently and safely. Our lives need the same balanced approach, especially in times of change and uncertainty. We must learn to deal with the

'fluctuating rotor blades' of life like health, family, relationships, work and integrating all experiences.

V. <u>Complete recovery is doubtful in case of power failure.</u>

Helicopter pilots know to minimize their time in the 'dead man's zone.' This aptly named realm of flight is clearly diagrammed in the flight manuals to warn pilots that in the event of a power failure in this 'height-velocity' zone, complete recovery is doubtful making the risk of crashing high. To escape and avoid the zone, one must keep a certain airspeed and altitude for safe operation. Be ready for autorotations just in case the unexpected happens.

<u>Spiritual application:</u> Stay focused yet expect the unexpected. Like hitting the unsafe area of flight, you'll stumble along the way and give up, turn back, or stray off course. It's easy and common to run into obstacles that slow your airspeed and altitude: jealousy, anger, impatience, negativity, misperception, unrealistic expectations, greed, and material concerns are typical. You get what you pay attention to, so stay focused on building awareness, trust, and faith that the Spirit connection is a most rewarding life. Don't give up, instead keep in mind that a 'power' failure along the way may be just the experience you need to teach you a valuable lesson in resilience or love. It could be a signpost helping you along the path. All experiences are beneficial.

VI. <u>A few misplaced pounds may exceed the design limits of your controls</u>.

Helicopters can be very sensitive to weight and balance and changes in the center of gravity (CG). Longitudinal (front to rear) center of gravity is more crucial than lateral. The helicopter can be loaded so that the CG ends up outside either the forward or aft limit. In most cases this may not pose a real problem with a slight nose-down attitude or more nose-up in forward flight.

<u>Spiritual Application:</u> Don't overload or overwhelm yourself. Integrate, process, and reflect that awareness will keep you from exceeding your personal "center of gravity." That doesn't mean never leave your comfort zone – those excursions can be filled with

opportunity and reward. But have in your spiritual tool kit practices that help you keep a peaceful center, always.

VII. "I think I can make it" is on the list of famous last words.

Helicopter pilots are a very competitive, 'can-do' bunch. Tell a helicopter pilot to go from A to B in the worst conditions and he will figure out a way to get there. It's in his nature. The mature pilot knows that like his machine he always has limits 'Know thyself and your machine' is a very good axiom here.

Spiritual application: The ego is always ready to take charge but that can be like handing the car keys to a six-year old. Do not let your ego push you to exceed your ability to learn, be open, trust, be humble, allow, surrender and be a vessel for Spirit to guide and work through you.

VIII. Make all approaches into the wind.

Helicopters depend on the wind for a stable landing and during takeoff for safety and to conserve power.

Spiritual application: Conserve and manage your energy levels. Use all the resources available to you. TAKE TIME FOR AURIC MAINTENANCE and rest.

IX. Avoid tail low attitude while near the ground.

Hitting the ground with the tail rotor not only can cause a hole in the ground but also causes serious control problems, and can ruin your whole day.

Spiritual application: Stay focused; avoid complacency and know your limits.

X. Safety dwells with the safest man who flies his helicopter as safely as he can.

Spiritual application: Know yourself. Check in with your higher self and Spirit in your daily choices. Ask for help, and listen for guidance, when you need it. You are never alone!

XXIII

You came out of the Universe at this precise moment
To contribute your unique gifts
To the great unfolding of the Universe.

I remember one day asking Sam to show me how to create a future reality where I was living a life with an awakened heart, and had successfully mastered all of my lessons and was living my true purpose. He laughed, and said, *That all? Aren't you there yet, pal?*

That's the great thing about this life, it's always shifting and I am always learning. Since I'd spent some time exploring spiritual practices, I was familiar with past life regression and how one could journey back into past lifetimes to heal karmic issues. Sam had assured that it wasn't just a one-way street back. I could, with the new energies, travel forward in time and create a vision of a future life that I'd want. I could even bring back the energy of that future lifetime to heal and accelerate my spiritual growth.

So, I decided to give it a go.

I meditated about connecting and merging with my higher self and set an intent to bring back a life that was loving, peaceful and nurturing and where all my desires come true. (Honestly, wouldn't everyone want that?) I envisioned what that life would look like and began to feel as if this reality had already materialized.

I began to create this vision using light energy like a child painting a picture. I drew in my mind the people, experiences, and environment I wanted. It was beautiful, Light-filled and harmonious. Then, I brought the energy of this future life into my DNA by imagining it changing my frequency and vibration at a cellular level. I radiated this energy through my body, emotions and mind. Finally, I imagined that years have passed and that I am my future self and living in this future reality.

It's now March 10, 2037. I am celebrating my 83rd birthday and soon my 50th wedding anniversary to my adored and lovely wife. My life couldn't be any better although I'm still learning and trying new things. Okay, I am moving a little slower now, but staying active. My life and body reflect the natural progression through the seasons of life with a heart full of love and gratitude.

It's been over 20 years since I last saw Sam. Of course, we still have our daily conversations, sometime, it's at 3 a.m. Our relationship has grown to new levels. I still ask questions on many issues -- politics, the weather, the afterlife, my writing, whatever, and he always chimes in with his keen advice and sense of humor. I am grateful for his wisdom and guidance. I'm getting better at listening and following his direction.

Robert...do you remember the time we...

Much has changed in my world since, most importantly, how I see my life and my spiritual growth. My life is filled with more joy, renewed purpose and expanded states of consciousness. I consciously pay attention to 'now' and living in love and awareness of our Oneness. Although, yes, I'm still on earth, I try to choose more heart-centered responses to my problems such as love, compassion, gratitude, cooperation, joy and others. My greatest source of contentment, is that I've completely accepted who I've become and acknowledged my mastery. This was my greatest challenge. There's no striving to be perfect anymore, I am also channeling the Archangel Gabriel and sharing her message of love and light.

Sam once said, it's not about trying to be perfect or how evolved you are or what you should be *doing*. Instead, it's loving yourself where you are and knowing that the inner wisdom of the Higher Self within is guiding you.

Flying With My Higher Self

Laugh more, relax and let go of judgments *and* not being in a rush to get to the other side.

You already know what the multidimensional experience is like Robert, he would remind me!

He reminds me of the reason that I am still here--to continue to release judgments and learn compassion for self and others, and integrate all my life lessons, and to help others on the path to mastery, and most important, to bring joy into my life. Joy and happiness go together, he says.

He also tells me that I'm here to witness the unfolding of the 'New Earth,' what he calls *the greatest show in the galaxy*! It's an enormous shift in consciousness since 2012 that is now reaching full potency culminating in the return of light in 2038. It's an energetic transformation on the planet and the opening of a new harmonic portal that is uniting humanity in unconditional love and light.

Of course, we're still experiencing the polarization inherent in the 3rd dimension - the war, starvation, pollution, genocide, conflicts, and chaos. But, there's also an awakening. People are becoming more aware of their spiritual natures, and that they are co-creators of their own experiences in the 'University of Earth.' It's a spiritual awakening on a global scale never seen before. Humanity can now explore higher dimensions much more easily. People are *becoming* their higher selves. We star seeds, are becoming the way-showers, healers helping others with their personal transformation and the Earth in preparation for the Ascension.

Sam and I are also planning our next life together. Not sure where that will be—back to earth, another planet, maybe in another galaxy or universe. My soul resonates with the calling to assist others in their quest for a deeper connection with the higher aspects of themselves. Perhaps this is my work in my next life.

Sadly, Gabriel and I are no longer together. I sold her to a helicopter enthusiast, a member of the Bell 47 Helicopter Association with the mission to protect and preserve the legacy of the Bell 47. Hard to believe that like me, she's on her 83rdth birthday! I will miss her.

Robert R. Maldonado, PhD

Recently, I saw her picture, on the Association's website, at a Northeast air show sitting next to a U.S. Marine Corps Sikorsky CH-53K, an 88,000 pound, giant. Looked like bookends for me and perhaps a message from Sam. I also got a nice letter from Gabriel's owner recently, and enclosed in it was a recent picture of Gabriel. When I turned it over I noticed the handwritten note,

I am glad that we found each other! We are together forever!
———*Gabriel*

It recalled a picture of me standing in front of MH-53J PAVELOW special operations helicopter tail # 4-4434, the last one I flew before retiring from the Air Force. It's beautiful message is still etched in my memory:

*"**My dear child, I held you and your comrades under my wings,**
Guiding and protecting you for over 40 years,
Vietnam, Grenada, Panama, Bosnia, Haiti, Iraq, Afghanistan,
On countless missions and always brought you home.
I stand here in quiet retirement in tribute to you,
And the Air Commandos of Air Force Special Operations,
And your motto: Any time, Any Place.
Go in Peace."*

Epilogue

Masters chart their own destiny and become a mirror of their higher self.

In the end, what I found from my conversations with Sam was that I had met myself, and that the answers to all my questions about mastery and the spiritual path had always been within me. *I Am My Higher Self.* The self-evident truth is that I wrote this book to remind myself and others of what it feels like to bring the Higher Self into one's life—the "US" relationship and, that we are like the pilot in the parable, having *conversations with our higher self, and in doing so we awaken to self-mastery.*

As Sam would say, that's how the game is played!

Once upon a time, a helicopter pilot came to earth and proclaimed to be a master teacher of the Truth that humanity can realize their God-Nature by becoming their Higher Self.

The pilot realized that he was to help others become the pilots of their lives—to help them move forward on their journeys with love, compassion and confidence—and to trust that the flight plan of their lives will unfold as it should.

Robert R. Maldonado, PhD

And, he traveled to different places and offered "Free Rides to the Ancient City" and there were some who went with him and were changed forever, for he loved greatly and felt compassion to those who suffered and could not find the love and light in themselves.

And, he vowed to leave the story of his friendship with Sam to the world for he knew that as he was changed forever, that others would be too.

Listen to and trust the guidance in your life and follow its voice. You'll become acquainted with spiritual things in a way that was impossible without it. You are the pilot of your life and are never alone.

Note to reader: As I read through the manuscript for the usual editing and structure, I discovered that it was incomplete. By this I mean that awakening to self-mastery on a spiritual path is an individual journey of transformation and that the experience is unique to us. Basically, we write our own script towards mastery. I am convinced that is what we are here to do. I've presented here my own experience, which I am hoping will serve a higher purpose for others in their own journey of learning and evolution.

I have also found after each reading that it is written on an infinite number of levels, as if my higher self wanted me to embrace a new way of knowing. Each time I read it I find a better and more comprehensive understanding of complex concepts, yet have more questions that need answers, perhaps for another book. Hopefully you'll resonate with some of the concepts and questions, even developing some of your own. I invite you to discover this for yourself as I did. Sending all of you many blessings!

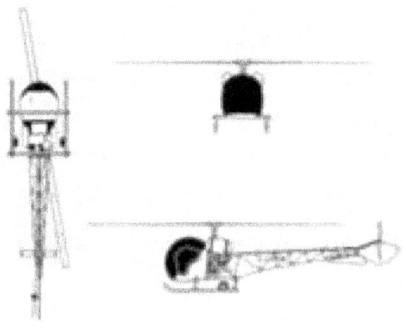

Resources

Flight Manual Bell Helicopter Model 47G-2 (1957).

NATOPS Flight Manual CH-53D Helicopter (1983).

USAF MH-53J Flight Manual (1994).

Bach, R. (1977). *Illusions: The Adventures of a Reluctant Messiah*, New York: Dell Publishing.

Coyle, S. (1996)—*The Art and Science of Flying Helicopters. Iowa*, Iowa State University Press.

Joyce, E. (2014). *Opening To Your Intuition and Psychic Sensitivity*, Pennsylvania. Visions of Reality.

Kennedy, W., & Kenyon, T. (2013). The Great Human Potential: *Walking in One's Own Light*, Canada: Ariane Books.

Kenyon, T., & Sion, J. (2013). *The Arcturian Anthology*, Washington: Orb Publishing.

Miller, D. (2013). *Arcturians: How to Heal, Ascend, and Help the Planet Earth*, Arizona, 3LightTechnology Publishing.

Padfield, R. (2014*). Learning to Fly Helicopters,* (2nd ed.), New York. McGraw-Hill

Roman, S. (1989). *Spiritual Growth. Being Your Higher Self,* California: HJ Kramer, Inc.

St. Germain, M. (2009). *Beyond the Flower of Life: Multidimensional Activation of Your Higher Self, the Inner Guru,* New York: Phoenix Rising Publishing.

St. Geramain, M. (2017). *Waking Up in 5D--A Practical Guide to Multidimensional Transformation,* Vermont: Bear & Company.

Thesenga, S. (1994). *The Undefended Self: Living the Pathwork of Spiritual Wholeness,* Pathwork Press.

Tyberonn, J. (2015). *2038 The Next Quantum Leap,* Arizona: Star Quest Publishing.

Walsch, N. (2017). *Conversations with God, Book 4, Awaken the Species,* Virginia: Rainbow Ridge Books, LLC.

Zellea, W. A. (2015). *Being a Master in the New Era: Integrating the Codes of Ascension,* Happy Awareness Publications.

Zellea, W. A. (2012). *Ascension Messages from the Higher Realms,* Happy Awareness Publications.

Glossary

Fifth Dimension—a vibrational frequency of unconditional love with the absence of fear, where compassion rules the emotions. It is what traditional religion would call heaven, where all aspects of self are fully integrated and expressed through the higher self. It is inner focused, Christ consciousness.

AFCS (Automatic Flight Control System) -- A system installed to improve the handling characteristics of the helicopter.

Ascension--A spiritual acceleration of consciousness, which allows the soul to return to the higher realms, freeing it from the cycle of karma and rebirth. It is a transformational process reached through the integration of the physical, emotional, mental and spiritual that allows one to transcend the limits of the third dimension and move into a higher realm.

2012 alignment—a time prophesied in the Mayan calendar when the earth came into alignment with the center of the Milky Way galaxy.

Akashic Records—the non-physical records of all past lives and the destiny of your soul.

Arcturus—a giant star about twenty-five times the diameter of the Sun and 100 times as luminous in the constellation Bootes, approximately forty light-years from earth.

Aura—the energy field that surrounds human beings and is seen in various colors.

Autorotation—a maneuver associated with flying and landing without power from an engine.

Bell 47G-2- a two-bladed, single engine, light helicopter manufactured by Bell Helicopter. The helicopter entered civilian and U.S. military use in 1946, in a variety of versions and designations for three decades. More than 5,600 were produced.

Chakras—the seven energy centers or "wheels" of the human energy field, each one is related to one of the physical organs of the body.

Collective—The control in a helicopter that controls the amount of blade pitch where all of the blades are varied in pitch and equal amount. It is also known as the power lever.

Cyclic—A control in a helicopter that changes the pitch of the rotor blades during each cycle of rotation. The cyclic is used to control the tilt of the tip path plane.

Height velocity Curve—the curve defining the area within which it is difficult or impossible to make a safe landing following an engine failure.

Hover—maintaining zero speed with respect to the ground.

MH-53J Pave Low III--was the largest, most powerful and technologically advanced transport helicopter in the world. The Pave Low's mission was low-level, long range, undetected penetration into denied areas (behind enemy lines), day or night, in adverse weather, for infiltration, exfiltration, and re-supply of special operations forces worldwide. The Pave Low system included terrain-following and terrain avoidance radar, forward infrared sensor, inertial navigation system with global positioning system, projected map display and suit of interactive defensive avionics systems enabling the electronic counter-measures and warning systems. A telescopic refueling probe on the starboard fuselage enable the MH-53 to refuel in-flight from the MC-130E/H/P/W series of airborne tankers. Two 450 gallon jettisonable external fuel tanks, one fitted to each side of the fuselage, extend the Pave Low's range out to 900km.

Running landing—a landing with groundspeed at touchdown.

Trim—with reference to controls—when the pilot is not required to hold a force on the controls to maintain them in position.

Website Reference

http://someinterestingfacts.net/wp-content/uploads/2012/12/How-to-fly-a-helicopter.jpg
Flying A Helicopter

Arguably the **most versatile vehicles used on Earth**, helicopters are used for military, civil and industrial purposes, offering unrivalled flight dynamism.

Helicopters consist of a large airfoil (a rotating blade assembly) mounted via a hinged shaft to an aircraft fuselage, engine and flight controls. Unlike fixed-wing aircraft such as planes, however, the flight principles of helicopters differ markedly, with their power emanating from the rotating motion of the airfoil instead of the plane's fixed wings and turbofan jet engines. Indeed, the fact that helicopters obtain lift from this cyclical motion complicates things massively, as it is directly affected by the horizontal or vertical movement of the vehicle at all times.

For example, in a plane the flight path of a wing is fixed in relation to its forward flight, while in a helicopter the flight path advances both forward and backwards through the circulation process of the rotors, with generated thrust parallel and in the opposite direction to it at 90 degrees. Therefore, when a helicopter is hovering in a stationary position, the plane of rotor rotation is directly parallel to the ground, balancing the helicopter's weight and drag with its generated perpendicular thrust/lift. In order to move forward, backwards or side to side, the helicopter therefore tilts the plane of rotor rotation (ie, the opposite direction to that of produced thrust) in that direction.

Complicating this process, however, are the effects of the rotor's opposite torque reaction, which due to the high rpm speed rotates the helicopter's fuselage in the opposite direction to that of the spinning blades. This is controlled by the addition of the helicopter's tail rotor, which is manually controlled by the pilot with the anti-torque pedals located in the cockpit. By adjusting these pedals the pilot can increase, decrease or neutralize torque dependent on the required maneuver.

In addition to variable rotation planes and torque reactions, helicopters are also subject to a 'gyroscopic precession' effect, a dissymmetry of lift caused by its forward movement. This occurs because as the rotor rotates while the helicopter is moving, the blades at the fore of any single cycle combine both their own velocity with that of the movement, while those at the rear of any cycle hold the difference between their velocity and the movement. This, in simple terms, means that the blades at the front move quicker than those at the back, producing more lift. If left unchecked, the helicopter would roll, so this is counteracted by altering the blade's individual angle of attack (the angle between the helicopter's lifting plane and oncoming flow of the atmosphere), decreasing that of those advancing and increasing those retreating to generate equilibrium.

Flying a helicopter is significantly harder than piloting a plane, due to the increased number of control inputs that need to be coordinated. There are four flight control inputs: the cyclic and collective controls, as well as the anti-torque pedals and throttle. The cyclic control – the joystick that sits between the pilot's legs – alters the pitch of the helicopter's rotor blades cyclically, allowing the pilot to change the rotor's thrust direction and overall vehicle tilt. For example, if a pilot pushes the cyclic stick forward then the rotor disc does also, creating forward thrust. The collective control is positioned to the left-hand side of the pilot (in a hand break-type position) and when risen changes the pitch angle of all main rotor blades collectively, independent of their position, increasing or decreasing altitude.

Flying With My Higher Self

Anti-torque pedals are positioned at the pilot's feet and control the direction of the helicopter's nose when pushed. These work by adjusting the pitch of the tail rotor blades, increasing yaw (rotation around a vertical axis) either to the left or right, dependent on which pedal is pressed. Finally, the throttle control – which is usually positioned as a twist grip on the collective control –affects the amount of power produced by the helicopter's engine, directly affecting the rpm speed of its rotors. Professional pilots must be trained to utilize them simultaneously.

(retrieved from http://someinterestingfacts.net/how-does-a-helicopter-fly/)

Archangel Gabriel

Gabriel is the only Archangel depicted as female in art and literature, Gabriel is known as *the messenger* Angel and is one of the four Archangels named in Hebrew tradition. Gabriel is considered one of the two highest-ranking Angels in Judeo-Christian and Islamic religious traditions. Apart from Michael, she is the only Angel mentioned by name in the Old Testament.

Gabriel is a powerful and strong Archangel, and those who call upon her will find themselves pushed into action that leads to beneficial results.

Gabriel can bring messages to you, just as she did to Elizabeth and Mary of the impending births of their sons, John the Baptist and Jesus of Nazareth. If you are considering starting a family, Gabriel helps hopeful parents with conception or through the process of adopting a child.

Contact Gabriel if your Third Eye is closed and your spiritual vision is therefore blocked.

> If you wish to receive visions of Angelic guidance regarding the direction you are going in.
> If you wish to receive prophecies of the changes ahead.
> If you need help in interpreting your dreams and vision.

Gabriel helps anyone whose life purpose involves the arts or communication. She acts as a coach, inspiring and motivating artists, journalist and communicators and helping them to overcome fear and procrastination.

Gabriel also helps us to find our true calling. Ask for Gabriel's guidance if you have strayed from your soul's pathway, if you wish to understand your life plan and purpose. She can also help if you can find no reason for being or if changes are ahead and you need guidance. If you are contemplating a house move, major purchase or thinking of changing careers.

Call Gabriel if your body is full of toxins and needs purifying and if your thoughts are impure or negative and need clearing and cleansing. Gabriel is also very helpful for women who have been raped or sexually assaulted and feel dirty as well as being under psychic attack or if you feel that you have absorbed someone else's problems.

(Reference: www.angelfocus.com/archangels.htm)

Your Higher Self

The term *Higher Self* has as its basic premise an eternal, omnipotent, conscious, and intelligent being who is one's real self. Each and every one of us has a higher self. Your Higher Self is, in simple terms, the highest aspect of you that can be attained and held in the physical body. It is the part of you that knows, sees, and understands at the highest level possible, while the physical part of you still continues to move around in the third dimension. Anchoring the wisdom of the Higher Self into your physicality is very much a part of our human spiritual evolution and purpose.

In recent years the New Age faith has encouraged the idea of the Higher Self in contemporary culture, though the notion of the Higher Self has been interpreted throughout numerous historical spiritual faiths.

In the Christian interpretation, all beings contain a fragment of the Holy Spirit, which ties them to their Higher Self. Christian theology adheres that the Higher Self is what connects one to God, and thus one must honor and keep one's Higher Self pure by following the ethical guidelines outlined in the scriptures. Christians serve God by realizing Christ as your Higher Self.

In Buddhism, the Nirvana Sutra describes the notion of Higher Self.

In Hinduism, the Higher Self is one and the same with the Jiva or individual's self. The Hindu faith teaches that the Higher Self, or "atman" is not an object possessed by an individual, rather the self is the subject that perceives. Hinduism teaches that through the examination of self-knowledge, or "atma jnana," one can attain salvation by comprehending the true self.

In the New Age literature, the Higher Self is viewed as an extension of the worldly self to a godlike state. It teaches that in exercising your relationship with your Higher Self, you will gain the ability to manifest your desired future before you. In other words, the self creates its own reality with in union with the Higher Self. They co-create together.

The *Pathwork of Self-Transformation* defines the higher self as our personal embodiment of and connection to the Universal Spirit through all things. It is the expression of God within, whether experienced on the personality level as an opening to love and truth, or on the transpersonal level as the inner teacher, spirit guides, or the immortal Soul, or on the intuitive level as cosmic consciousness.

Meeting the higher self is the human experience of ourselves as filled and flowing with Spirit, the life-force, or God. It is known as *coming home to our true identity*, by remembering who we really are. The vibrations of the higher self are always pleasurable, reassuring and heart-warming. In its presence, we feel a quickening of life energies. We feel invigorated and renewed. The quality of the finer *higher self energy* is of relaxed activity, harmonious movement; along with a trusting and loving attitude, ease and self-assurance.

About The Author
Robert R. Maldonado, PhD

Robert Maldonado

Robert Maldonado is an energy healer and teacher who has dedicated himself to helping others discover their innate healing abilities and guiding them through life transitions. He has experienced many life transitions and roles himself as a student, husband, chemical sales-engineer, flight instructor, military officer and pilot, public school teacher, martial arts instructor, counselor and healer.

He is a retired U. S Air Force lieutenant colonel having spent the majority of his professional career as a U.S. Marine Corps helicopter pilot, and with the elite "Air Commandos" of the Air Force Special Operations Command.

Robert R. Maldonado, PhD

A former Command pilot with over 3,000 flight hours and squadron commander, he has flown the TH-57, UH-1E, T-34B, T-28B, CH-53A/D (Marine Corps); HH-53B/C, and MH53H/J (Air Force) aircraft.

Upon retirement, he taught elementary and middle school U.S. History and Mathematics before retiring from Fairfax County Public Schools in Virginia. He has lived in Germany, Venezuela, Peru, Mexico and has traveled the world and has a passion for discovering the beauty and honoring the sacred in all places and cultures he has visited.

Robert is also a Certified Energy Medicine Practitioner/Instructor; Certified Healing Touch Practitioner; Barbara Brennan Healing Science Practitioner, Reiki Master Teacher; Shamanic Practitioner, Quantum Touch practitioner and a teacher of Integral Chinese Qigong and Tai Chi. He holds a PhD in Energy Medicine from Akamai University specializing in Spiritual healing and additional certifications in Education (K-8), Judo, Jujitsu and is an ordained minister and Siddha in Transcendental meditation. His academic background includes a PhD in Systems Analysis from Columbia Pacific University, PhD in Theocentric Psychology from La Salle University, and graduate degrees in education, business, religion, international relations, and psychology.

He is the author of *"The Calling of the Heart: A Journey in Self-Healing"* describing his personal experiences in transformation and healing, weaving together wonderful teachings from his life and journey's in Peru, South Africa, Australia, New Zealand and Canada as an energy healer.

Additionally, he is the author of *"My Maori Experience: New Zealand 2007, A Spiritual Journey to the Sacred Land of Mystical Peru, 2008";* and, *"A Healers Journey: My Return for the Deactivation of the 20th Special Operations Squadron and the Retirement of the United States Air Force MH-53M PAVELOW Helicopter."*

Other published works include: *"Counterinsurgency: Realities and Alternatives";* and *"Planning the Air Campaign in Unconventional Warfare Operations"* in Spanish while a United States Air Force Special Operations exchange officer with the Peruvian Air Force.

Robert has published his first novel, *"Children of Atlantis: Keepers of the Crystal Skull"*, an Indiana Jones style metaphysical adventure about an archeologist who discovers an ancient crystal skull on the bottom of Lake Titicaca only to find out that he about his past life in Atlantis. His destiny is to open sacred sites around the world using the skull for the ascension of the planet. Being pursued by the forces of darkness he invites the reader to follow him through his journal entries as he tries to explain how it all began and why he finds himself on his current quest.

This novel also allowed Robert an opportunity to connect with the land of his childhood and rekindle those magical, transcendent and healing memories.

Robert is currently on the faculty of Akamai University as an adjunct professor of Complementary and Alternative Medicine and works as a writer, healer, and teacher. He resides in Fairhope, Alabama with his wife Ellen, dogs Buddy and Blue, along with their cat, Maggie.

www.ingramcontent.com/pod-product-compliance
Lightning Source LLC
Chambersburg PA
CBHW070537170426
43200CB00011B/2458